NERO'S
WATCHING
VIDEO

NERO'S WATCHING VIDEO

GARTH HEWITT
— WITH MARTIN WROE —

Hodder & Stoughton

LONDON SYDNEY AUCKLAND TORONTO

This book is dedicated to my mother –
Daffodil, and to the memory of my
father – Thomas.

British Library Cataloguing in Publication Data

Hewitt, Garth
 Nero's watching video: troubadour in a
 troubled world.
 1. Christian life
 I. Title   II. Wroe, Martin
 248.4   BV4501.2

 ISBN 0 340 41034 5

Contents

NERO'S WATCHING VIDEO

Nero's watching video while Rome begins to burn
Nero's wearing roller-skates so he can quickly turn
And get away from what he doesn't want to see or want to
    hear
Nero's wearing headphones and they stretch from ear to ear
Nero's got a private world for which the heart may yearn
Nero's watching video while Rome begins to burn

Nero lives the lyrics he hears in every song
Nero is the hero, Nero's having fun
Nero's going crazy, Nero's going blind
He's fed too much on fantasy, he's somehow crossed the line
Nero can you hear me
Is there anyone inside
Nero keeps on laughing
So no-one knows he's died

    Nero's watching video while Rome begins to burn . . .

Tension on the TV, a world out of control
Wounded people weeping never touch his soul
Nero's changing channels, Nero's moving on
Nero's feet are moving to a very different song
Nero can't you hear them
Don't you ever feel the pain
The sounds go through his ears
But they never touch his brain

    Nero's watching video while Rome begins to burn . . .

He's moving out, he's moving up, he's always moving on
Nero moves his body to a thousand disco songs
Nero is the product of an advertiser's dream
He took in all their slogans, he's part of the machine
Nero do you realise
There's another world outside
Where the poor keep getting poorer
And the hungry have just died

    But Nero's watching video while Rome begins to burn . . .

Nero's watching video, Nero's at the disco
Nero doesn't want to know, Nero's watching video

Preface

This book was due to be finished in '84 – but I'm glad it wasn't written on schedule. Since then there have been trips to Kenya, the Sudan, Poland and a tour of the US, plus return visits to Uganda and India. All have played a part in shaping this book. The tour with Scripture Union called 'The Bride' at the time of the miner's strike, the 'Broken Land' tour of Ireland in '86 and working with Jim Wallis of the Sojourners' Community in '86 also played their part in shaping my thinking.

There are so many people to thank. Many I have mentioned in the list at the back and thanks to all of those who were my companions on the journeys. There are many more who have given me time and hospitality and have helped me understand the warm character of our compassionate and just God. They have taken time to show me their city, village or refugee camp. They have welcomed me in their homes – whether in a shanty town such as Crossroads in South Africa, a refugee camp in the Sudan or in the villages of India, Africa or the Carribean. I have glimpsed peoples joy and had a brief insight into their pain. It has made me a more passionate person. I realise my understanding of the gospel is deeper – my commitment is stronger – I hope this book nudges people to a closer understanding of the character of our caring God.

In the poor and oppressed I have seen His face and I have not remained the same. I am no longer entirely at ease in Western society when I know it is built on injustice. But in Jesus I find hope – hope that we can start to change our society with His help. The tide often seems to be running the other way – it is not fashionable to be compassionate. But as G. K. Chesterton points out 'only the Church can save us from being a child of our times' and that is part of the freedom and hope of the gospel.

Escapism is the temptation for the Christian. Nero may have fiddled as Rome burned – today there are many temptations to keep us away from facing reality. The rising threat of the so-called 'prosperity doctrine' is just one anaesthetic to stop the two edged sword of the gospel cutting through.

Special thanks go to Sue Elkins who typed all the manuscript for me (twice) and gave me very helpful advice as well as contributing her poem that 'says it in a nutshell' for the beginning of chapter nine; and to Martin Wroe who also spent days of hard work sifting the material and helping me to get a better perspective on it. He helped to accelerate the work at a significant time and joined me for part of the 'Broken Land' tour. Although he can't stand being described this way – he was an important catalyst – and I'm very grateful.

Martin told me the preface is where I thank him for doing a wonderful job and point out that all the good bits are mine and any mistakes are entirely his – at least I think that's what he said – very kind of him, I thought.

Thanks also to Jane Stevens, my secretary, to all the Greenbelt executive committee, to the trustees of the Amos Trust and all those involved with its work. Also to my prayer support group, to George and Pauline Hoffmann, Steve Rand and all at Tear fund, Tony and D'reen Neeves, John and Linda Muggleton and all at Greenleaf, Bill Latham and Cliff Richard, to David Bracewell and the congregation of St. Saviour's Guildford, and special thanks for support from the family at crucial times – to my mother, Grandma and Grandpa Sumner and to the Colonel and his Lady!

Finally my daughter Abi described the preface as 'that front bit where you thank us for putting up with you while you were writing it'! She has a knack of hitting it on the head – so very special love and thanks to Gill, Tom, Ben, Abi and Joe, who've had to put up not only with the writing of the book but also with the times away that sparked it off. So, thanks for your love – for all the fun, for keeping me sane and for the boxed Bruce Springsteen set for my 40th birthday!

Gill has borne the brunt of this book and the trips behind

it. I've returned exhausted and exhilarated, shocked, inspired or just plain ill and she's never quite sure what to expect! Thank you for your constant faith and encouragement.

(Preface written in Nelson, South Island, New Zealand on Tuesday 5th May '87 while on Tear Fund New Zealand tour, 'A Future and a Hope'.)

TROPICAL NIGHT

Tropical night – it's a beautiful sight
I can hardly believe I've arrived.
Tropical night – grips you so tight
making you feel so alive.

Tropical sounds – echo around
sounds that are new to my ear.
Tropical sounds – keep your ear to the ground
there's a feeling that just could be fear.

    Oh I see beauty all around me
    But I see pain in every face
    Romantic dreams – they're gone completely –
    they can't survive in such a place.

Tropical night gives way to the light
A beautiful nightmare comes in.
Tropical tears with topical fears
about what tomorrow may bring.

    Eyes that hunger for affection
    hands that reach out like a prayer
    empty plates and empty pockets
    tell a tale we seldom hear.

Tropical night – something's not right
somebody's playing with your soul.
Tropical tears – feeding on fears
with never a chance to grow old.

    Eyes that hunger for affection
    hands that reach out like a prayer
    empty plates and empty pockets
    tell a tale we seldom hear.

Tropical night – it's a beautiful sight
I can hardly believe I've arrived.
Tropical night – grips you so tight
making you feel so alive.

1. TROPICAL NIGHT – Haiti

'The question to be asked is not what we should give to the poor? but when will we stop taking from the poor?'

Jim Wallis

'If you put an end to oppression, to every gesture of contempt, and to every evil word; if you give food to the hungry and satisfy those who are in need, then the darkness around you will turn to the brightness of noon.'

Isaiah 58:9–10 (GNB)

'The Christian gospel is a two-way road. On the one hand, it seeks to change the souls of men and thereby unite them with God; on the other hand, it seeks to change the environmental conditions of men so that the soul will have a chance after it is changed.

Any religion that professes to be concerned with the souls of men and is not concerned with the slums that damn them, the economic conditions that strangle them, and the social conditions that cripple them is a dry-as-dust religion. Such a religion is the kind that Marxists like to see – an opiate of the people.'

Martin Luther King Jr

Port au Prince

As we flew in low to Port au Prince airport, I marvelled at the beauty of the Caribbean Sea and the island that lay beneath me. It was just before sunset, and even as we landed there were the hints of colour that come up in the sky and create those beautiful sunsets that are so much a feature of that part of the world. We had arrived in Haiti on the first leg of a journey that was to take in the two countries that comprise this one island in the Caribbean – Haiti and the Dominican Republic.

The very name 'Haiti' had an air of mystery about it for me. For a start, this was my first visit to this part of the world, and even as we flew in I'd just finished reading Graham Greene's book, *The Comedians*, which is all about Haiti and its capital city, Port au Prince. The echoes of that evil regime of the previous dictator Papa Doc are never too far away.

The senses always seem particularly alert when arriving in a new environment. There are new sights, new smells, new sounds, new feelings. We had just flown out of a British winter – this was January 1978 – and so the very feel of warmth that hit us as we got out of the aircraft changed our mood almost miraculously. Dusk came quickly, and as we drove for the first time through the crowded streets of Port au Prince the sights and sounds had a mystery and almost a romance about them.

That first night I didn't sleep very well, and at three o'clock in the morning I got up, having been disturbed by sounds outside the window. I was surprised to see a steady stream of people walking down into the capital city, all carrying loads on their heads – a stream that seemed to go on endlessly. I discovered later that they were heading for market and that they had to set off in the middle of the night in order to get there on time.

My visit to Haiti was on behalf of Tear Fund, a Christian relief and development agency. They had invited me to look at projects in Haiti and the Dominican Republic that are particularly related to children. The following year had been designated the International Year of the Child and they wanted me to write some songs for a new audio-visual in relation to this. Consequently we spent much of the trip in schools, hospitals and children's homes and also out in the villages and in local homes seeing how people lived and what sort of problems they had to face day by day.

I realised on going to Haiti that I would see poverty. What surprised me, though, was the quantity of poverty. The first morning we were driving through what I took to be the shanty-town area of Port au Prince; it seemed to go on endlessly, until it gradually dawned on me that this was the normal condition for most people in that city. Poverty was the status quo in Haiti.

I still retain vivid, colourful images of that morning. In one place a man shinned up a palm tree and brought down a coconut for us, skilfully chopping the top off to enable us to drink the coconut milk. Another man invited us inside his hut to inspect his family shrines – a rather dark and gruesome experience in the land of voodoo. Image after image tumbled through my mind that morning – moments of humour, moments of sadness, moments of poignancy, often not knowing quite how to react as I experienced for the first time the warm welcome, the life and the vibrancy of the Third World, coupled with the poverty, the pain and the deep suffering.

Port de Paix

From Port au Prince we travelled up north to Port de Paix where, nestling just off shore, is the island of Tortuga, reputedly the ancient hiding place of pirates and buccaneers. The journey may have been little different from travel generally in the Third World – as we bounced along on the roughest of roads and haggled with the locals for help when badly swollen rivers halted our progress – but for me it was utterly new and fascinating.

After a very long journey we eventually arrived and stayed with some Christian workers linked with a hospital there. I sang to some of the workers that night at an informal gathering.

One of the people we met at Port de Paix was an American pastor. When I sang on our first night to a group of workers from the hospital and mission he was there. He asked me if I had a relative called Thomas. It was so out of the blue that I was somewhat taken aback. 'Yes,' I replied, 'my son is called Thomas.' 'No,' he responded. 'Someone older.' I told him that my father had been called Thomas. 'Did he ever write a commentary on the epistle to the Hebrews?' he asked. 'Yes,' I replied. 'I am currently teaching the book of Hebrews to the people here,' he explained, 'and it's your father's commentary that I'm using.'

It was a special moment. I had flown further away from home that I had ever been before. That day I had just travelled an unbelievable distance to a village of mud huts, to discover that my father's commentary was being used to teach people. My father was a Geordie coal-miner when he became a Christian. He had gone into a Christian meeting with a gang to break it up. What happened that night at the meeting no one really knows, but suffice it to say that my father was a changed man from that day on. He travelled a long road before writing that commentary. He stayed working in the pits for some years, later becoming ordained as an Anglican minister. From being poorly educated he had gone on to master Greek, Hebrew and Latin. It was a thrill for me to hear of his book being used up there in the village of Port de Paix, just as much as it was for my mother when later I passed on the news.

On the beach

The next day we spent wandering around the village of La Pointe. The poorest section of the village was in fact the beach. It was an exotic and beautiful beach, the sort of place that would normally be turned into a tourists' paradise, yet for these people it was where the poorest tried to eke out a living and survive – living in little shacks and lean-tos. Here I met Pierre, who tried to make his living from collecting almonds. Pierre had almost no possessions and lived in a little shack with his wife, yet through his ragged appearance a real dignity shone, and he talked in an animated way about his faith in Jesus Christ. When I sang that night to a large group of villagers in the local church, he was in the front row clutching his most treasured possession – his Bible.

16

As we walked along the beach, we marvelled at how beautiful it was, and yet what pain and suffering it contained. Somehow the photographs could never capture this because all they show is an exotic tropical beach. We are conditioned by tourism to look in only one way at these sort of sights. Of course, it's beautiful by any standard, but it is no good simply marvelling at this beauty if we fail to see the ugliness that is created when people are being deprived of their natural dignity as human beings by the circumstances in which they are forced to live.

Haiti is in fact the poorest country in the western hemisphere. It is an ecological disaster area because so many trees have been cut down for burning in order to create charcoal for cooking, but this in turn has meant that the wind has swept away the topsoil and turned a Garden of Eden paradise into an arid wilderness.

We are tomorrow's world

On our way back to Port au Prince we passed some workers in a field. The men were digging and hoeing, while the women danced and sang. It was all done to a simple chant and evidently the women were – to everyone's amusement – improvising verses about men who were slacking. It created a wonderful atmosphere and everyone moved to a rhythm, whether dancing or working. The sheer community spirit and enjoyment in the work was great to see. I took the simple chant they were singing and put a single sentence to it – 'We are tomorrow's world.'

I had to record something for Tear Fund's audio-visual that they had tentatively entitled *Tomorrow's World*. It was a filmstrip about their work for children. I took the tune to a school for blind and handicapped children, and there we recorded the song with them. They sang it with incredible enthusiasm, led by a Stevie Wonder lookalike on the congas. Tony Neeves of Greenleaf Advertising was Tear Fund's producer for the audio-visual, so he was recording the song. After about fifteen minutes he said he had enough. Getting them to stop was another problem, though. They just kept right on singing. Eventually I resorted to shouting 'Stop!' at the top of my voice, but it only seemed to raise the excitement. For all I know they may be still singing it today!

Hispaniola

After Port au Prince we then headed to the Dominican Republic. Though I remember singing at several schools in Santo Domingo and the surrounding area, my memory is slightly blighted by the fact that I was ill for most of my time there. The Dominican Republic seemed to be a country very different from Haiti, even though it was part of the same island, because it looked much more to Latin America and was much more Latin in style. Even the children didn't join in the songs in the schools in the same way, whereas in Haiti they sang with a power and a force that I've only encountered in one other place – Uganda.

Haiti, or Hispaniola as it used to be known, was visited by Columbus and then by the Spanish *conquistadors*. During the first fifty years of colonisation, one million Indians – almost the entire indigenous population of Haiti – were annihilated by being turned into slaves. They simply could not accept the indignity of being made slaves, so they died out. France took over the island a couple of hundred years later and brought in slaves from Africa, and so the Haitians are basically African people. Treated harshly as slaves, they eventually rebelled, and on 1 January 1804 they proclaimed an independent Haiti and claimed that they were the first black republic in the world.

You will never forget

The last night I spent in Haiti was in Port au Prince, where I talked with Wess Stafford, who works for Compassion, an American development agency. He said to me, 'You will never forget what you've seen here,' and he added: 'What's more, you must never be silent about it. On every album you make and at every concert you do, you must say something about our responsibility to the developing world.'

For me he seemed to speak with a prophetic voice. In fact, ever since then I have always included a song or two with this emphasis, both in albums and concerts, because I felt that I had had this privilege of seeing at first-hand the incredible injustice there is in our world that forces so many people into circumstances of deep material poverty.

Yet at the same time I have come to value the riches of the Third World – riches in terms of culture, community life, and often spiritual life – which we in the West need so much. 'It is more blessed to give than to receive': this truth has become more and more relevant to me. It is nowhere more important than in regard to the issue of our attitude to the so-called developing countries. It's so easy to paint a picture of people living in poverty and starvation and to end up with a caricature of these countries which implies that the people themselves have no dignity and nothing to offer, and that we are the only ones who can help. Of course we do have material resources that can help, but our world is unjust in the way it shares the resources that are available. Any society that can spend increasing quantities of money in developing nuclear weapons – and can use the best scientific brains of our world to create more and more evil ways of destroying one another while large sections of the globe are in such poverty – is clearly one that is riddled with problems.

A variety of culture, the warmth and strength of community life and family life, the depth of Christian faith: these are all things from which I have grown richer as I have travelled on these journeys to places of material poverty. That night in Port au Prince in January 1978 was a night of commitment for me, where I promised that I would not keep quiet about what I had seen. Strangely enough it wasn't the start of a journey – I think that as we look back we can see God's hand at work, drawing together strands and threads right through our lives that lead us to where we stand today.

Martin Luther King

As a teenager of sixteen years old, one Sunday afternoon I went up to St Paul's Cathedral and heard a sermon that Martin Luther King preached before he went to Oslo to pick up the Nobel Peace Prize. I remember what a profound effect this had on me because of his very complete presentation of the gospel.

His sermon was on the subject of right relationships, and his text was Revelation 21:16: '. . . its length and breadth and height are equal' – words from John's vision that refer to the new Jerusalem. King said that the new city God was building would not be an unbalanced entity with caring virtues on one side and degrading vices on the other. The most noble thing about it would be its completeness, whereas the troubles of our world are due to incompleteness. He went on to show that the length of someone's life is their understanding of themselves and their discovery of self-fulfilment. The second dimension, he said, is the breadth, which is the concern for and identification with one's fellow man, the recognition of the oneness of humanity and the need for active brotherly concern for the welfare of others. And the third dimension is the height: he said that a man must actively seek God and that the only way for us to know him is for Jesus Christ to be Lord of our lives.

He ended up by saying, 'Love yourself, if that means healthy self-interest, this is the length of life. Love your neighbour as we are commanded to do, this is the breadth of life. And the greatest commandment: "Love the Lord your God with all your heart, with all your soul and with all your mind and with all your strength," this is the height of life.' It seemed to me then, and it still seems to me now, to be a very complete presentation. Ever since then it has affected my thinking, my reading of the Bible and, hopefully, the way I live.

Amos rides again

Back in 1973 I started writing songs with this kind of emphasis, one of which even contained a reference to

Martin Luther King, 'The People of the West (Amos Rides Again)'; another, called 'Walk in His Shoes' (see chapter eight), became the title track of a film-strip for Tear Fund.

'The People of the West (Amos Rides Again)' was so titled because of the impact on me of the prophet Amos. The book of Amos starts in a dramatic way with the prophet pointing a finger at countries far away from Israel. One can almost hear the applause. As his criticism falls on their close neighbours that applause seems to get louder. But then there is a deafening silence as he speaks God's judgment on Israel itself — because they 'oppress the poor and crush the needy'.

The relevance of this prophecy to our own western way of life struck me very forcibly, and it has a particular challenge for those who claim to be Christian or 'religious'. God says through Amos, 'I hate, I despise your religious feasts; I cannot stand your assemblies' (Amos 5:21). Why? — because 'You trample on the poor . . . You oppress the righteous . . . you deprive the poor of justice' (Amos 5:11–12). 'But let justice roll on like a river, righteousness like a never-failing stream!' (Amos 5:24).

A vicar wrote to me after hearing 'The People of the West' and said I was a 'communist dupe'. He had entirely missed the point of the Amos reference. The challenge of Amos to his own society was powerful and pointed, but he had already spoken of the injustice of other societies. In other words, it is easier to see the faults of others than it is to see our own, but injustice is still injustice wherever it occurs. To criticise our own society is not to endorse another where the criticism is just as valid.

The People of the West
(Amos Rides Again)

You've silenced your prophets
You've shot down your dreamers
Your life-blood is money
You're exploiting the poor.
Oh the people of the West just love to invest
In the system that keeps the poor man poor.

21

You have no compassion
Your lifestyle is evil
Higher living standard
The God you adore.
Oh the people of the West just love to invest
In the system that keeps the poor man poor.

But let justice roll on like a river
Truth like an ever-flowing stream
Then tears of rage will turn to laughter
And people become what they should be.

You ignore the ways of justice
Though you talk a lot about it
You victimise the stranger
Seeking refuge in your land.
Oh the people of the West just love to invest
In the system that keeps the poor man poor.

Greed is your mother
Silence is your father
Your epitaph is written
In frustrated tears of rage.
Oh the people of the West just love to invest
In the system that keeps the poor man poor.

But let justice roll on like a river
Truth like an ever-flowing stream
Then tears of rage will turn to laughter
And people become what they should be.

Living the gospel

It is curious how the church has been able to duck the issue
of social justice at various times in its life and development,
because when we read the Bible it is quite staggering to
observe the strength of its commitment to justice and
righteousness. God is a God who is utterly committed to
both. We are called upon to obey him to reflect his attitude
in the way we live. Yet most of the time we ignore the
incredible divisions there are in our world and do little to be
the reconciling and healing forces, despite this challenge at
the very basis of our Christian belief. If we believe we are

made in the image of God, then so too are the hungry and the oppressed, wherever they are to be found in our world – whether it's the Caribbean, Africa, Latin America, the Philippines, Asia, Afghanistan or in the urban areas of Western Europe and America. Poverty and injustice exist in every land and in every society, and the Christian is called to be consistent in speaking out against injustice and showing a community that is committed to justice for the poor and oppressed.

The very way we live says something about our theology and our attitude to life. If we live as if we believe that people are not of value in God's eyes, then we must not be surprised if people don't take our Christianity seriously. We cannot preach the gospel unless we are seen to be living the gospel. We can't say that we love God with all our heart unless we are seen to be concerned and doing something about loving our neighbour as ourself, whether that neighbour is in the inner cities of this country or in one of the so-called developing countries. After being in Haiti, I remember thinking about the word 'love', of how often it's a word that's romanticised. Yet it's a word in the Bible that is linked with the word 'obedience'. If we love God then we'll seek to do what the prophet says in Isaiah 58:6. 'Remove the chains of oppression and the yoke of injustice, and let the oppressed go free' (GNB).

After Haiti, Wess Stafford's words constantly echo in my ears: 'You must never be silent about what you've seen.'

Romantic images disappeared in Haiti and I heard the cry, not for pity but for justice.

> I see beauty all around me
> But I see pain in every face
> Romantic dreams – they're gone completely –
> They can't survive in such a place.

RAINBOW OVER KAMPALA

Night-time in Kampala
Can't believe my ears
Night-time in Kampala
You can almost smell the fear
The guns they play a sad tattoo
Out on the street tonight
Night-time in Kampala
Tell me who put out the light.

Day-time in Kampala
Can't believe my eyes
The beauty of the city
Peeps through a sad disguise
The cars they weave a drunken path
Through the pot-holed streets
Day-time in Kampala
Nothing seems complete.

    But I have seen a rainbow over Kampala
    I have seen a sign of hope
    In a city that will change
    Angels fly low over Kampala
    Waiting for the moment the healing will begin
    Oh I believe I can hear them start to sing.

Jesus in Kampala
His love is reaching out
Jesus in Kampala
I've seen him there's no doubt
I've seen him in his followers
And the way they live their lives
Jesus in Kampala
The sign that hope survives.

    But I have seen a rainbow over Kampala . . .

The Father is watching his children tonight
His diamond-studded eyes
Gleaming wet with the sight
The tears that he sheds
Are for the healing of your land
The rainbow is a sign
That you're always in his hand.

    Oh I have seen a rainbow over Kampala . . .

2. RAINBOW OVER KAMPALA – Uganda

'Peace is not automatic. It comes when hearts are exposed to the love of Christ. But this always costs something. For the love of Christ was demonstrated through suffering, and those who experience that love can never put it into practice without some cost.'

Festo Kivengere, Bishop of Kigezi, Uganda

'The God of the Bible is the God of liberation rather than oppression; a God of justice rather than injustice; a God of freedom and humanity rather than enslavement and sub-servience; a God of love, righteousness and community rather than hatred, self-interest and exploitation.'

Allan Boesak

'What is impossible to man
Is possible with God'

Song of Misaeri Kauma, Bishop of Namirembe

Entebbe

It was June 1982 and I was flying from Jomo Kenyatta airport in Nairobi, heading to Entebbe. 'Entebbe' – a word that sparks off a thousand memories, with the amazing Israeli raid, which in turn sparked off an apparently endless stream of films. 'Entebbe' – by that one incident perhaps one of the most famous airports in the world.

As we flew closer a battle ensued between my mind and my stomach. My mind was marvelling at the beauty of Lake Victoria below me. My stomach was suffering from unpleasant heaving as a reaction to the air turbulence that we were hitting which so often accompanies flights in this part of the world.

Soon we were actually standing at Entebbe airport and being met by Bishop Misaeri Kauma, a friend of mine who had organised this tour of Uganda for me. Misaeri and his wife Geraldine had been long-time friends from my university days in Durham, and fourteen years previously had invited me to visit Uganda for concerts. I hadn't exactly forgotten about it, but I had certainly shelved the idea because of the difficulties that Uganda had been experiencing, particularly during Idi Amin's time. I met up again with Misaeri in the autumn of 1981, when he repeated his invitation – only this time it sounded to me more like a command! I said I would try to come, but it didn't seem very feasible at the time. But with the cooperation of African Enterprise the finance was found and I set off with a team which included Richard Bewes, the Chairman of African Enterprise in the UK and now Rector of All Souls' Church, Langham Place; Lillian Clarke, our guide and 'roadie', and a great asset to our journey (though in her mid-seventies, Lillian outstripped us all in energy and enthusiasm); and also Dave Hofer, who brought in our thirteen cases of sound equipment. These cases proved among the most valuable assets of the trip. I ended up singing to audiences that were frequently several thousand strong in huge, often open-air venues where the value of a good PA system could never be overestimated.

Light in darkness

Uganda was exhilarating. It was challenging and, at times, frightening, yet I came away from that short visit feeling that I had been deepened in my faith, and that somehow I had grown up a little.

Uganda is a country of enormous potential and yet at that time it was a country that was not at peace. Just before I went on the trip, I read an article in the *Guardian* newspaper written by a couple of American journalists. They had been in Kampala two weeks before we were due there. They had been arrested and imprisoned briefly, and they headed their article, 'Horror Story from Africa's True Heart of Darkness'. It ended with these words:

> Today in Uganda five main tribes regard each other with at best suspicion, at worst hatred. For eight years Uganda suffered the iniquities of Idi Amin. Today its President, Dr. Obote, makes only rare public appearances, protected by machine guns. Today Uganda is Africa's true heart of darkness. (The *Guardian*, 22 May 1982)

That is one side of the picture — a country that has suffered terribly through Idi Amin's regime and has never fully recovered, and a country that has suffered further massacres through Milton Obote's time. When a country descends to the rule of the gun, it's a hard rule to change — particularly when many people can make their living by the simple use of it. So corruption and violence had become a way of life in this land. Curiously it is not this side of Uganda that sticks in my mind when I think of that visit. It is of light shining in that darkness. This light came from the lives of certain individuals I met whose Christian faith was so real and so marked by joy — not a superficial happiness but a joy always born out of suffering. It seemed there was no one there who had not had suffering come very close indeed. If they had not suffered themselves, somebody in their family or among their close friends had.

We were given a tremendous welcome at Entebbe airport, and the first concert was in the town of Entebbe itself. I sang, Richard Bewes spoke, and we experienced the people's incredible enthusiasm that marked every aspect of this trip. There was an obvious enjoyment of music and its rhythm, but also a great hunger to hear about the Christian faith and its reality and hope in a situation which for them was so often hopeless. It was always hard to finish concerts as people wanted more and more. The longer a meeting or concert went on, the more people arrived, and one of the problems of our trip was that each day we had at least three different events. Actually managing to get from one to the next proved a major problem – not just because we had to go on longer than expected, but also because of the sheer welcome and hospitality that we were shown in every place. Before I'd even sung a note at Entebbe, one local clergyman came up to me and said, 'The very fact that you are here encourages us, because it lets us know that we are not forgotten.' That comment spoke volumes to me.

Roadblocks and violence

After the concert at Entebbe, we drove to Kampala, passing our first roadblock. Roadblocks became a feature of this trip. They were manned by the army, but in most cases the army were not actually paid and so they made their living from roadblocks. Consequently each roadblock was a threat. For the local Ugandans it could be a place where they were robbed or beaten up; it was a place where some people lost their lives. We reckoned we passed about a hundred roadblocks during our short visit, which gives some indication of the daily insecurity with which the Ugandans have had to live. On a recent return visit, in October 1986, it was a welcome relief to find President Museveni's army so much more disciplined at the roadblocks.

As we arrived at Misaeri Kauma's house in Kampala – in fact, just as we were greeting Geraldine – we heard the sound of shooting for the first time. Misaeri told us not to worry, and we went inside. In Kampala people tended to get indoors each night at about seven o'clock because it was then too risky to be on the streets, and several nights while we were there we heard the sound of shooting in the distance, and sometimes very close at hand.

A large part of our trip we spent in the Kampala area, and therefore these recollections reflect the insecurity of that town at that time. It does not necessarily represent the situation as it was throughout Uganda. Since then the situation has often been even worse, but certainly in the autumn of 1986 there was a marked improvement.

On our visit we did concerts at schools, colleges, at

Makerere University, and in the churches and cathedrals of the area. We also did programmes for Ugandan TV and radio. Indeed our arrival in the country was announced on the national TV and radio news. Nowhere in the world have I known such a reaction to the music. The moment I started playing, the whole crowd would seem to move, and their singing, as they joined in the choruses of the songs, had to be heard to be believed.

It was a trip marked by contrasts of emotions. One morning we visited Makerere College School. It was without doubt for me one of the highlights of the visit – a quite incredible sense of excitement accompanied our entrance into the hall, and the response to the concert was electric; it was one of those moments one wished could have been captured on video. We returned to Misaeri's home for lunch, full of enthusiasm, only to meet tragedy: a local archdeacon was there to tell the bishop that a vicar and his wife and one of the leaders of a church had just been shot dead. The archdeacon's own situation was difficult enough as he had had to leave his own area and was now living in a garage underneath his daughter's home.

I found this the most emotional moment of our trip, being torn from one mood to another as the excitement of that morning evaporated and the bitter tragedy of everyday life, which is replayed again and again, registered on me. Ugandans have had to live with this all the time, and it made me very conscious of the life-and-death urgency of the Christian message. No wonder people listened so intently to a message of hope in a situation like this. Our world is scarred and in so much pain, but the message of the gospel is one of healing and reconciliation in a divided world, of right relationships being restored to a community, of right relationships being restored with God; a message of healing in a world that hurts, a message of hope in a world that is so often hopeless. We have light to bring in darkness because of the light of the one who is the light of the world. Forgiveness and reconciliation are just two aspects of the gospel that is so desperately needed in Uganda.

The father's song

That night I sang to the clergy of the diocese, including the previous Archbishop of Uganda. It was at the time of day just before they would all have to leave and get back to their own homes. It is an evening I won't forget.

I sang a song called 'The Father's Song', which is based on some words from Psalm 46 linked with words of Revelation 22:

> Be still and know that I am God
> I stand among you, and I am God
> Though the mountains crumble and disappear
> I will be with you, you need not fear.
>
> There's a river of joy flows on and on
> Flows through the city, it's the Father's song
> There's a tree of life by the riverside
> The leaves are for healing where the tears have been cried.

It's a song I had written a few years earlier, after a visit to Belfast, and as I sang it that evening, I got them to join in. After a while I brought it to a conclusion – but they asked me to sing it again, and to keep singing. Suddenly the song spoke more forcibly to me, and I realised why they wanted to repeat it and learn it. We need to capture a vision of the greatness of God in a situation like that and to have confidence in him that, regardless of what happens to society and to our world, he is bigger than those situations and he gives us strength to do the right thing in the kind of uncertain life that so many of these people had to lead, where they were dealing with daily tragedies and traumas.

In this context we saw the unity of the gospel as expressed by people like Bishop Misaeri Kauma and Bishop Festo Kivengere. There is no divide between social action and the proclamation of the gospel. The gospel *is* helping the widows and orphans, it *is* helping the refugees, it *is* proclaiming a message of forgiveness and peace, it *is* introducing people to Jesus Christ, it *is* helping to heal the wounds of a scarred society, it *is* a commitment to justice and to truth, even when there is a cost in standing for these things.

The revolution of love

One incident occurred that – like a parable – focused the difference that the gospel of peace can make. We were told about a large house in Kampala where one of Idi Amin's men lived. It was used to kill people and torture them. It had a fearful reputation – people were even fired at when passing the house. After the fall of Idi Amin the house was taken over by African Enterprise. They painted over the very dark and morbid interior and from a house of darkness it became a haven of light. When I was shown around it they took me to a little store room which had been used as a cell to intern, torture and kill people. There had been blood stains on the floor when they first arrived in the house. As I peered into this little room – now used to store books – the first thing I noticed was a book by Festo Kivengere entitled *The Revolution of Love*. 'That', I thought, 'sums up the changing power of the gospel' – from a way of hatred to a revolution of love.

South to Kabale

After Kampala we headed off south to Kabale at the invitation of Bishop Festo Kivengere. We crossed the equator and passed through the towns of Masaka and Mbarara. We were now retracing the route in the opposite direction that the Tanzanian army had taken when they marched into Uganda to remove Idi Amin. The towns still showed the effect of the devastating bombing that occurred at that time. They had been more or less flattened before the army came in. This journey brought home to us some of the lack of resources that was so commonplace in Uganda. One of the problems was simply finding petrol. There was no petrol at all in Masaka, although we managed to find some in Mbarara and eventually drove up to Kabale.

It was a memorable situation that greeted us at Kabale, as a crowd of about three thousand were waiting for us. By then they had been waiting there for three hours as we were running very late. Bishop Festo had been pleading with them to go home, but they refused, saying, 'They will arrive,' and just waited. The welcome we received, and the attentiveness and the enthusiasm of the audience were once again thrilling to experience. Only the onset of darkness ended this particular concert, but they came back at lunchtime the next day for another one.

Our visit in this part of Uganda was short, but I appreciated having done it as it stressed to me the sheer natural beauty of the country, which in that mountainous area looks almost like Switzerland and would be a major tourist attraction were it not for some of the difficulties that Uganda is experiencing.

Up in this part of Uganda, you are not far from Rwanda and Tanzania, and recently in his diocese Festo has had some of the camps full of so-called displaced persons – people who do not even qualify to be called refugees, who have been put in camps on the border of Rwanda and Uganda – people rejected by both countries. He has been deeply involved in the battle to draw the world's attention to these people and to bring basic supplies of food and medicine to forgotten people.

We stood at the front of Festo's house, looking out over the beautiful hills, on the morning that we stayed there. I asked him about his own experiences of fleeing across those same hills when he knew that Idi Amin was after him to take his life, and how he felt having to leave not only his home but also his diocese. As he talked, just for a moment I sensed the pain and horror of such a time.

Namirembe

As a result of my Ugandan visit I wrote two songs, both of which were really a tribute to some of the individuals whom I met in this country and whose Christian faith was such an encouragement to me and helped me to understand the breadth of the gospel of peace and justice. (It would, incidentally, be wrong to paint too glowing a picture of the church in Uganda. Like the church in every country, there are problems and tensions, there is corruption and there is

32

dishonesty – but in the midst of this there are examples of true shining faith born out of suffering.) One song was called 'Rainbow over Kampala', a prayer for that troubled city, and the other was called 'Namirembe'. Both titles were suggested by Richard Bewes, who nagged me until they were written!

The word 'Namirembe' means 'hill of peace', and on this particular Kampala hill is the cathedral. As you travel around in the troubled city you can see Namirembe with its cathedral on the top. It seemed to me it was almost a symbol of hope, a symbol of the possibility of peace in this wounded city. As I discovered the meaning of the word Namirembe, it reminded me of another hill of peace – the hill of Golgotha, where Jesus died, which stands as a symbol for our world of the possibility of peace in a scarred, wounded and broken society, and as a reminder to Christians that we are not called to opt out of society but to be part of the reconciling, healing, forgiving, proclaiming community which shares the love of Jesus in word and deed.

When I was in Kampala a recollection of the first time I'd heard of the hill Namirembe often came to mind. In fact, it was when I read *Janani*, the story of Archbishop Janani Luwum, who was killed during Idi Amin's time. I remember reading, and being very moved by, the story of the funeral: how thousands had gathered on the hill Namirembe, devastated that even their archbishop had now been killed. At the funeral they had no body – the government wouldn't give his body back – and people were simply standing there, mourning. Then the old archbishop came out – Erica Sabiti – and began to read the story of the resurrection, in particular the passage where the angel speaks at the tomb of Jesus, and says to the women, 'Why do you look for the living among the dead?' (Luke 24:5). Spontaneously a song of praise was taken up around the hillside – 'Glory, glory, Hallelujah' – as people realised the relevance of this passage and as the message of the resurrection struck home to them.

When I saw Namirembe it seemed to me symbolic of the

possibility of peace and healing within society, and also a reminder of resurrection:

> Oh Namirembe
> Oh the hill of peace
> Oh Namirembe
> God's love will never cease.
>
> High up on the hillside its light cannot be hid
> The Cathedral is a symbol of the way that we should live
> High up on the hillside as a sign the time will come
> The kingdom is among us, keep following God's Son.
>
> Oh Namirembe
> Oh the hill of peace
> Oh Namirembe
> God's love will never cease.
>
> Jesus dying on the cross on another hill of peace
> A place of pain and agony to say the very least
> But it became the healing place from which all love does flow
> From His death there came new life that everyone can know.
>
> Oh Namirembe
> Oh the hill of peace
> Oh Namirembe
> God's love will never cease.
>
> Beat the drum, beat the drum,
> See the mighty warrior come
> Glorious at the setting sun
> The King has come to reign.

ROAD TO FREEDOM

The sights that fly before your eyes
Can simply drag you down
I lived a year in Calcutta
The night I hit town
Those sights you see – they freeze your brain
You can't even say a prayer
But they don't need my pity
They don't need my sympathy
Let each one have his dignity
And a chance to be on the road.

On the road to freedom
On the road to freedom
Let the poor man stand up tall
Give him back his pride
On the road to freedom
On the road to freedom
Give him back humanity
Let him know his worth
In his Father's eyes

And in Calcutta late at night
A million coal fires burn
Smoke gets in your throat and eyes
And heart and soul in turn
Your spirit weeps at pain-filled streets
'I never knew' I cry
But they don't need my pity
They don't need my sympathy
Let each one have his dignity
And a chance to be on the road.

On the road to freedom . . .

God's Spirit is upon me now
So Jesus told them all
Because He has appointed me
To bring good news to the poor
He sent me to bring liberty
To set the captive free
To fight against oppression
Poverty which is aggression
To bring righteousness and beauty
And a chance to be on the road.

3. ROAD TO FREEDOM – India

'The second I met Mother Teresa she struck me as being the living embodiment of moral good. I felt I had no business sitting beside this tiny giant. There was no false modesty about her and there was a certainty of purpose which left her little patience. But she was totally selfless; every moment her aim seemed to be, how can I use this or that situation to help others. She was never pious about this . . . She is one of the few people who have impressed me on sight. I was in awe of her. She held my hand as she left and said, "Remember this – I can do something you can't do and you can do something I can't do. But we both have to do it."'

Bob Geldof

'The righteous will then answer him, "When, Lord, did we ever see you hungry and feed you, or thirsty and give you a drink? When did we ever see you a stranger and welcome you in our homes, or naked and clothe you? When did we ever see you sick or in prison, and visit you?" The King will reply, "I tell you, whenever you did this for one of the least important of these brothers of mine, you did it for me!"'

Matthew 25:37–40 (GNB)

Long years ago we made a tryst with destiny and now the time comes when we shall redeem our pledge . . . at the stroke of the midnight hour, while the world sleeps, India will awake to life and freedom. A moment comes, which comes but rarely in history, when we step out from the old to the new, when an age ends, and when the soul of a nation, long suppressed, finds utterance . . .

So spoke Jawaharlal Nehru to the Indian Constituent Assembly on 14 August 1947, on the very eve of India's independence.

It was freedom that was the theme very much on my mind during my first visit to India in November and December 1982, not least because 'Road to Freedom' was the title already given to me by Tear Fund for a roadshow I was to do following the tour. Also in preparation for my visit I had read the book *Freedom at Midnight*, Larry Collins and Dominique LaPierre's fascinating account of India's struggle for independence.

I was gripped by this story and by the natural and compulsive desire for freedom from colonialist rule that pervaded it. I found the description of the movement for independence genuinely moving, as the Indian Poet Laureate proclaimed in New Delhi on 15 August 1947: 'O lovely dawn of freedom that breaks in gold and purple over an ancient capital,' and as the crowds chanted, 'The British are going. Nehru is going to raise a new flag. We are free!'

But freedom is always costly and it is always a struggle. India's own road to freedom was and is fraught with difficulty, not least with the painful amputation of West and East Pakistan (now Bangladesh) – with its conflict between Muslim and Hindu that necessitated this, and the current conflict between Sikh and Hindu.

The battle for freedom, it seems, is one that never ends, and yet that struggle is vital because freedom restores to a person and to a nation their dignity.

Calcutta

There is not much dignity, though, for those who live and die on the streets of Calcutta – treated by the world as if they are of no significance. It was seeing them and then meeting Mother Teresa that sparked off the lyrics to the song 'Road to Freedom'.

Visiting Mother Teresa was a highlight of my trip to India. I took my guitar with me because I wanted to sing her a song I'd written back in 1973 called 'Walk in His Shoes' which had adapted some of her words. (See chapter eight for lyrics.)

In fact the whole song was something of an adaptation: her words were an adaptation of Matthew 25, and the chorus of the song was my adaptation of the words of Jesus, which in turn he had adapted from the prophet Isaiah! I had at the time of writing the song received permission to use Mother Teresa's words, but I imagined that she would never have heard the song.

Unfortunately, on the day of my visit, the sisters had undertaken a vow of silence. Mother Teresa was happy to chat, but she expressed considerable disappointment that I couldn't sing to the sisters, and even for a moment seemed to toy with the idea of lifting the vow – I was glad she didn't, though. I would have been sorry to have been the cause of breaking such a worthwhile spiritual discipline.

The meeting was very important for me because it was a moment of great joy. Calcutta had been a tremendous shock. The sight of thousands living and dying on the streets has a depressing impact and I remember feeling stunned, not quite knowing how to cope with such a situation.

In my discussion with Mother Teresa, she talked about the first quality that she looked for in her sisters – joy. She told me that they must have a cheerful disposition, it was no good having people who were easily depressed as there was enough depression in the streets of Calcutta. She needed people who would bring hope. The very atmosphere that surrounded their work spoke of joy and peace and hope in a city which too frequently signified the opposite. As we talked together, Mother Teresa described her work among the destitute and the dying in a memorable phrase: she spoke of giving 'dignity to the poor'. It was a phrase that was to stick strongly in my mind.

As we walked back to the car after our visit, I remember saying to Steve Rand of Tear Fund and Tony Neeves of Greenleaf – my companions on this trip – 'Now I've found the theme of the song that I'm going to write.' And so dignity to the poor became the theme of the 'Road to Freedom' song:

On the road to freedom
On the road to freedom
Let the poor man stand up tall
Give him back his pride
On the road to freedom
On the road to freedom
Give him back humanity
Let him know his worth
In his Father's eyes.

The way we behave shows how we value people, and if we allow them to be left in conditions that suggest they are simply objects or that they don't matter, then we deny the value and worth of human beings as made in God's image. I believe it is impossible for somebody to understand the love of God until they can actually see this love in action. If someone has never been shown a loving act, how can they possibly believe that there is a loving God?

And the good news for the poor, fairly dancing out of the pages of both Old and New Testaments, is that there is a loving God, but it is the members of Christ's body – his church – who have to show this love in action so that the possibility of belief can raise its head from the ashes of despair.

Meeting people in Calcutta whose lives shone bright with hope in a situation far too often dark with despair was a reminder of the light that is brought by the love of Jesus being shown in action. There were others I met who also showed me this hope.

One was Wai Sin Hu, who spent two days walking me round some of the poorest areas – there I saw overwhelming poverty. Wai and his wife Rose work with children and students, supplying them with food and education. Wai himself was born and raised in one of Calcutta's poorest localities, but despite successfully fighting for a proper education and thereby securing a rare escape route from the poverty trap, he felt compelled by the love of Christ to return to his roots and show the gospel in action.

Christian freedom is never an excuse simply to escape, rather it's the chance to show service, and Wai and Rose, to my mind, typified the Christian example of what it is to serve with joy.

There were other signs of hope that I saw in Calcutta, not least Vijayan Pavamani and his wife Premila and their lovely family. Actually it was Vijayan who took me to see Mother Teresa. He started the work of Samaritans in Calcutta and now runs a drug and alcohol rehabilitation centre called the Arunoday Mid-Way Home. I went up to visit the Mid-Way Home and to sing to some of the people there, and again it was a spark of hope, seeing lives that were changed and transformed.

Although the work of Wai and Rose, Vijayan and Premila, Mother Teresa and her Sisters, may not have changed the whole of Calcutta, it was an encouraging reminder that something can be done, and though you may not change the whole city, you can change the lives you touch. For me this was a strong antidote to the temptation to despair. Despair is the most crippling emotion of all, yet there is always that temptation to be overwhelmed and to feel helpless. To me they were examples of the right approach to discipleship – simply getting on and doing something, and thereby letting Jesus be seen on the streets of Calcutta. Of course, I'm sure there are many, many more, but these are the people that I met who reminded me of the way of Christ at perhaps one of the most traumatic moments of my life.

Drought in Tamil Nadu

From Calcutta we headed to the drought-stricken area of Tamil Nadu in southern India. Here, in a different context, again the theme of freedom came home forcibly to us. Talking with people, we discovered that there were wells in even the driest areas – indeed we had been puzzled suddenly to come across lush fields in the middle of the drought area. It was explained to us that the wells were owned by rich landlords who would only let the water be used in return for payment. This meant that most people had given their land to the rich landlords in return for water, and were now living on it as tenants. Then they were further obliged to work for the landlords at a pittance as bonded labourers – all in order to get the water needed for survival.

One day we were in a village called Villapakam when one of the EFICOR (Evangelical Fellowship of India Commission on Relief) drilling rigs hit water. It was our last day in the villages in India, and it was an exhilarating moment that I shall always treasure. The excitement in the village was intense.

The well had been drilled among the 'Harijans', the poorest people of the village. These were the people who in the old days were called 'untouchables', and Gandhi had given them the name 'Harijan', meaning 'children of God', to try and give value to people whose lot in life was always to be devalued. Even as EFICOR were drilling, they were berated by someone from a higher caste for not drilling among the upper-caste part of the village. The very act of drilling in that part of the village was a Christian statement to say that all people are valued and equal in the sight of God.

The joy as the water came bubbling out of the ground took on a deeper significance for me as I realised that not only was there now pure water that would be available in the village instead of a long walk away, but that at a deeper level villagers were set free from bondage to the rich landlords. It was in a sense a political act, an act of justice, an act of hope, as indeed all such acts that bring good news to the poor must be.

The high price of water

The high cost of water and the high cost of freedom were brought home to us in another village, Melputhupakam, not far from Vellore in southern India. In this village we met Lily, whose husband had been the village schoolteacher. They were both active Christians, and they were also Harijans. As we talked to Lily with an interpreter we discovered a most tragic story.

Naturally, as in so many other parts, the drought had affected their village, so water was strictly rationed. Many of the upper-caste people had pipe connections from the water tank to their own home, which meant that there was precious little water left for the Harijans who lived in a separate area away from the main village. They were also meant to be able to draw from two taps out of about ten at the main tank, but whenever upper-caste women came, they took precedence, and in the end the Harijans were virtually prevented from drawing water at all. This situation became a source of dispute.

In the end Lily's husband took the case to the District Collector, who represented the government. He said that in future the private water supplies to the high caste should be disconnected and all water drawn from a tank in the main village. The ruling naturally caused some resentment among the upper caste, and the Harijan women were constantly harassed and eventually physically prevented from getting any water at all.

Lily's husband went off to protest to the leaders of the main village, but such was the resentment of the upper caste that they came and beat him to death and burnt down the houses of the Harijans. Not only was Lily's husband killed, but forty-five homes were destroyed as the Harijans struggled for their rights within that village.

Once again EFICOR had been in and had drilled a well, but while we were there it was actually drying up. When we went to leave the village we were surrounded by the Harijan men. Their faces were a picture of absolute desperation. They thought we were there to drill the well, and they pleaded with us not to go. As soon as the well dried up, they explained, they would have to go back to the main tank. Then there would be another outbreak of violence, because they had been threatened that others would be killed if they used it. Fortunately Matthew George of EFICOR, who was with us, was able to guarantee that a team would come back and drill the well as an absolute priority. Later we were to hear the news that not only had they drilled a successful well, but the message added the lovely words, 'The people's joy knew no bounds.'

On my visit to India I was learning first-hand the desperate need for freedom from oppression. The oppression of injustice and poverty that stops people living as the complete human beings that God intends, the injustice that denies people their dignity as people made in God's image. Justice was a word that began to mean even more to me as I looked at the situations of poverty. It seemed inextricably linked with the word love and the Christian commission to love God with every part of ourself and to love our neighbour as ourself.

Floods near Karnpur

If freedom and dignity were the themes that particularly came out of the Indian trip, then it was water that constantly sparked them off – either the lack of it or, ironically, sometimes too much of it. Our trip started near Karnpur, in an area called Hamirpur, among some villages that had recently suffered flood disasters. Tear Fund was working in this area with local Indian agencies and had already given clothing and cooking utensils to people who'd lost everything in the floods. So often it is a drought area that is then affected by flooding. The ground is baked so hard that when the water comes sweeping through it takes everything in its wake and then within maybe even a few days people are back to a drought situation again.

The true spirit of Christmas

Hamirpur was an intriguing experience. We left England at the end of November, with the shops full of their Christmas decorations, and I remember thinking that I would hardly feel very much like Christmas in India. Yet in Hamirpur I was to realise how much closer I was to the true Christmas spirit. As we walked round one of the villages, it had a distinct nativity feel to it. Somehow it seemed much closer to the birth-place of Jesus, and as the animals shared the same building or part of the same building as the people, every corner seemed to be another scene taken from some Christmas tableau.

One of the people from the village told me that there had been a village on this spot for about eight thousand years. The way of life, he said, had hardly changed at all. It is still the same agricultural society, which made me realise that I was much closer to the kind of society into which Jesus was born. Strangely enough, we found we all became much more sensitive to the gospels as the relevance of the images that Jesus used somehow took on a heightened meaning because he was drawing them from a society that was so close to this.

Cyclone in Gujarat

From Hamirpur we went across to Gujarat, where there had been a cyclone not long before we arrived in India. Indira Gandhi, who was Prime Minister of India at that time, was appealing for relief agencies to visit the area and to help, so we went across to see the situation for ourselves.

I had never been into a situation where there had so recently been a disaster, and I saw some very tragic sights. Many villages had been devastated and probably over a thousand people had been killed in this particular cyclone. But one has to remember it is not only the deaths that are the tragedies, but also the fact that whole villages are made homeless, cattle are drowned, crops are destroyed, and people are left with absolutely nothing.

We spent some time in a village called Vankiya, where we met one man, Gobar Madha, who had an extended family of sixteen people. Fourteen members of his family had been drowned in a wall of water that went through the village as a result of the cyclone. He had saved the life of his little son, Gabaru, by holding him with his teeth as he himself hung on to a tree. We saw the scars of his teeth marks on his son's body. There is very little one can say in the face of such a tragedy. We simply sat with him for a time as the local village leaders explained to us what had happened. There are no easy or glib answers in a situation like this.

I wrote a song about the tragedies we had seen. They had all related to water – either too much or too little. The song started off with Vankiya village in Gujarat. Verse three was about Hamirpur and a conversation I had with a man called Gangararm who told me of praying for rain in a drought situation, and then experiencing the tragedy of flooding in which he lost all his possessions and only just saved his own life. The song ends in the drought region of Tamil Nadu in the south, where I had the experience of standing on a vast dried-up river bed and realising for the first time the devastating effect of the drought. All are scenarios that stay vividly with me.

Water, Water

Water, water everywhere
The wind is on the rise
Destroying all that's in its path
Before your very eyes.

Cyclone heading up the western coast   *Gujarat*
Who will it be this time?
Like a game of roulette the wheel is in spin
Like some dramatic sign.

Water, water everywhere
The wind is on the rise
Destroying all that's in its path
Before your very eyes.

Lives are lost – they count the cost
Houses swept away
Cattle are drowned, the crops are ruined
A legacy of pain.

Water, water everywhere
But who will get to drink?
Some are swimming with the tide
While others simply sink.

Flood waters come sweeping down   *Hamirpur*
You'd been praying for rain for days
Clinging to a roof top
Your possessions float away.

46

Water, water everywhere
But who will get to drink?
Some are swimming with the tide
While others simply sink.

Then I see the thirsty earth   *Tamil Nadu*
Cracked and sandy brown
Five years of drought have done their worst
No water to be found.

Water, water everywhere
But not a drop to drink
Water, water everywhere
What am I s'posed to think?

The mighty arches of a ghostly bridge
Mocked by the sun-parched land
Standing on the dried-up bed
Of a river that turned to sand.

Water, water everywhere
But not a drop to drink
Water, water everywhere
What am I supposed to think?
Don't it make you think
Who will get to drink?   © David Paramor Publishing

Returning home from India in mid-December, I was
plunged into all the pre-Christmas rush. I had sung my first
Christmas carol that year in Vankiya, Gujarat, the next at a
special concert I did in the chapel at the Vellore Medical
Mission Hospital. The style of the birth of the Son of God, I
knew, was much closer to what I had seen there than to
what I returned to in materialistic Britain. Yet this was
where I and Gill and the children all lived. Somehow I had
to link the two worlds, but it was not easy.

For five days I found I could not talk about what I had
seen, so great was its effect. Then George and Pauline
Hoffman of Tear Fund came and took Gill and myself out
for a meal. With his own experience in those situations,
George drew out my reactions, and to Gill's surprise I
began to unravel my thoughts and experiences, which I had
so far kept quiet about. Since then, we have as a family tried
to incorporate some of these experiences into our attitudes
– into the way we view the world and into the way we live.

In many ways, 1982 was the year that I felt I grew up, as I saw the struggle for so many people in Uganda and also in India: the reality of life as it really is for most people in our world – the daily struggle for freedom from poverty, for freedom from injustice; the daily struggle simply to get enough water to survive. Yet it was out of this very same sort of society that a man came saying, by implication, 'I am the water of life': 'If anyone thirst, let him come to me and drink. He who believes in me, as the scripture has said, "Out of his heart shall flow rivers of living water"' (John 7:37–38 RSV).

This can never become a reality until his people, the body of Christ, actually physically and practically bring freedom from oppression and poverty – and bring hope – into a world that is so often conditioned by despair. This can never be achieved simply by our words: 'Let your light so shine before men, that they may see your good works and give glory to your Father who is in heaven' (Matthew 5:16 RSV). If people see the love of Jesus in action, then they will know who he is and they will follow him. However many sermons are preached, people cannot believe if they cannot actually see the love of the Father. It's up to the body of Christ. We can hide him from people or we can make him clear.

> God's Spirit is upon me now
> So Jesus told them all
> Because He has appointed me
> To bring good news to the poor
> He sent me to bring liberty
> To set the captive free
> To fight against oppression
> Poverty which is aggression
> To bring righteousness and beauty
> And a chance to be on the road.
>
> On the road to freedom . . .

Postscript

In January 1986 I returned to India for a very different visit. It was at the invitation of a record company – Akash

Recordings. They had released my album *Alien Brain*, and they toured me with an Indian band. I played in Bombay, Poona, Madras, Kottayam, Goa and Delhi.

It was good to catch a glimpse of another side of India, to talk to young people who have a pride in their country and do not want it to be seen only in terms of its poverty. It is in many ways a country of the future, like so many Third World countries. Though it is a country with a long and ancient history, with its ever-growing population of close to eight hundred million, it is very much a country of the next century, and this is something you can sense.

The Third World is tomorrow's world. Now it may be struggling against the tide of poverty and against the inequalities of our world – the richer nations have stacked the odds in their own favour and often blatantly exploited the poorer nations – but this is not the end of the story. As we oppose the oppression of poverty, we must make sure that we do not simply pity and patronise, or view India simply in the light of its poverty. There is so much more to the story.

In Delhi I met the family of H. P. George; he was the man who took us to Hamirpur and Gujarat on my visit in 1982. A great worker for others, he could not be at my concert that night in Delhi as he was down in Bhopal trying to organise more support for the victims of that industrial tragedy. Perhaps the very fact that the Bhopal disaster happened at all shows how one half of the world fails to value the other.

LITANY FOR AFRICA

A man of God is weeping
He pleads to God in prayer
His people are the victims
Of government by fear
Of the iron fist of injustice
Of the bitter fruits of greed
He pleads to God for freedom
Outside his people bleed.

From Sharpeville to Soweto
Or down in Uitenhage
Crossroads or Guguletu
All feel the white man's rage
With guns and tanks and armoured cars
State violence goes unchecked
To keep the white man's burden
Upon the black man's back.

 This is a litany for Africa
 A litany for Africa
 A litany for Africa
 The wound has gone so deep
 God bless Africa
 Guard her children
 Guide her leaders
 And give her peace
 And Lord make us instruments of Your peace
 And Lord make me an instrument of Your peace.

He dug the gold and diamonds
He made a nation rich
She waited on their tables
But she never shared their dish
The broken heart of Jesus
Cries out in bitter pain
As injustice like a hammer blow
Nails Him up again.

He died to say we're valued
He died to show our worth
He died to say I love you
To every soul on earth
And every unjust system
Each evil deed that's sown
Each person who's devalued
Is another nail knocked home.

4. LITANY FOR AFRICA – South Africa

'None of us was prepared for the full reality of apartheid. As a contrivance of social engineering, it is awesome in its cruelty.

'It is achieved and sustained only through force, creating human misery and deprivation and blighting the lives of millions. The degree to which apartheid has divided and compartmentalized South African society is nothing short of astounding. We understood why many visitors to South Africa could leave the country enchanted by its natural beauty and impressed by its economic achievement, yet oblivious of the scale of the human tragedy behind the façade of progress. The living standards of South Africa's white cities and towns must rank with the highest any-where; those of the black townships which surround them defy description in terms of "living standards". Apart-heid creates and separates them; black and white live as strangers in the same land.'

Commonwealth Eminent Persons Group Report, *Mission to South Africa*

'You cannot reform evil, you've got to eradicate it. So far, all Botha is interested in is to make apartheid saleable. But you cannot come up with a better system of apartheid – apart-heid is apartheid full stop. The best way to make sure that Communism takes over South Africa is to perpetuate the system. Because I tell you, it makes Communism look very good.'

Caesar Molebatsi

'We must recognise that the motives and forces behind racism are the Anti-Christ, denying that man is made in the divine image.'

Bishop Trevor Huddleston

It was an item on television news that sparked off the first verse of 'Litany for Africa'.

The scene was one of violence in Soweto as the police clashed once again with the local community. Then the report cut to a church in Soweto where Bishop Desmond Tutu (just prior to his appointment as archbishop) was praying. His eyes were tight closed and yet tears poured down his face as he prayed, 'Lord, we know that one day we shall be free – but why does the cost have to be so high?'

Place names like Sharpeville, Soweto, Uitenhage, Langa and Crossroads all have that ring of the horror of injustice. Tragically it seems to be a list that keeps growing. As the black community calls for justice and freedom, the hand of apartheid strikes back more and more forcibly.

Apartheid, of course, is a system diametrically opposed to the Christian gospel. To support it is to deny the gospel, for in Christ the barriers of oppression and hatred come down. As it says in Galatians 3:28, 'There is neither Jew nor Greek, slave nor free, male nor female, for you are all one in Christ Jesus.' The old barriers of racism, oppression, sexism, are to come down. This is the work of the Prince of Peace – to bring right relationships.

Apartheid has exploited cheap black labour to build a society of wealth for the white few. It is exactly the kind of exploitation that made the Old Testament prophets howl. Yet apartheid has been perpetrated by a government that claims to be Christian: it is therefore a heresy. Because it denies the image of God in each individual, it spits in the face of God: it is therefore a blasphemy – an insult to God.

Recently a programme on Channel 4 called *Witness to Apartheid* began with the words of Archbishop Tutu: 'In South Africa it is not a question of civil rights, it is a question of fundamental human rights – the recognition that a black person is a human being created in the image of God.'

In March 1983 I visited South Africa for Tear Fund South Africa. I had been in black townships before. I had even seen the horror of Sun City standing like a golden calf of materialism – wallowing in its own self-indulgence – with a desert of poverty all around it. But in March 1983 I saw more, and then I realised that it is not enough simply to stick bandages on to wounds. To do this and to keep quiet is to endorse the status quo. There is a sickness at the very heart of the society, and it is disobedience to God and his laws.

Soweto

It was a rainy morning in Soweto – an unusual sight in a year of drought. It is actually a shock to drive down the road as I did that Monday morning, 7 March 1983, from Johannesburg to Soweto. In a matter of minutes you have driven from the first world to the Third World.

Soweto stands for 'South-Western Townships', and it is a dormitory town for Johannesburg, where the black labour that helps to produce the wealth on which Johannesburg and South Africa are built sleeps and lives. It is perhaps better off than most other townships because the riots in 1976 brought it to the eyes of the world. A lot of money has been ploughed into Soweto since then. Indeed, at the time I was there, the government presumably viewed it as a model township, as bus-loads of tourists were driven through to take a look at certain selected parts. About a third of the people at that time had electricity – indeed there were some houses in Soweto that were really very good indeed. However, what amazed me was – despite the attention of the world, despite the spotlight that had been put on Soweto – the appalling level of poverty that still remained. Of course, that Soweto exists at all is a profound injustice.

In a curious way, that Monday morning rain, pouring down and turning the streets into rivers, matched my mood. The sadness and pain of a separated society won't just go away, either because it's ignored or because the standard of living is raised. Injustice always remains injustice, and has to be rooted out.

Sadly, due to lack of support, Tear Fund South Africa no longer exists. But in 1983 the aim of my visit was to make an audio-visual and highlight some of their projects. We even started working on the filmstrip. It was to be called *Broken*

Land, but it was never finished. I was disappointed because the projects Tear Fund supported were some of the best that I had seen anywhere. Howard Cooper, who headed it up, was a down-to-earth straight-speaking person, and maybe his honesty lost them support. He refused to get a permit to go into the black areas as he was supposed to, since he felt this was endorsing the system. When he spoke in churches he was forthright in his condemnation of injustice and his support of the poor and the oppressed.

Travelling with Howard and with Tony Neeves of Greenleaf, my first stop was in a part of Soweto known as Meadowlands. It was clearly a very poor area; my only surprise was that it seemed exactly like so many other parts of poverty in the Third World, which one wouldn't expect in a country where there is so much wealth.

One of the schemes that we visited was helping people to grow their own gardens in Soweto so that they could produce their own vegetables and supplement their diet. Another project was a feeding scheme – necessary because of the malnutrition that existed in the area. In this particular section, several families shared one front door in blocks that had originally been built for the miners, and the conditions were obviously appalling. We also visited the only two existing children's homes in Soweto. More such homes were desperately needed.

Later that evening, I spoke to a group of university students at Witwatersrand University and told them of my experiences in other Third World situations – in India, Uganda, and then Haiti. They listened attentively and responded much as any other audience would. When I talked about what I had seen that very day only a few miles from where we were, the reaction was different. It seemed to be one of shock. When I talked of the poverty and the squalor and the bad sanitation in which people were forced to make their living, there seemed to be genuine surprise.

What people from outside South Africa often forget is that apartheid is a two-way thing. People don't cross the borderline either way. So often they genuinely don't know the whole story. After I had spoken and sung, the first comment from those students was, 'But we've never been there – we didn't know.' I am convinced that this is the excuse that many of us in Europe or the USA use about the injustices in the world. We say, 'Well, I haven't seen it, I don't know' or 'It's not really like that' or we quote someone who's been there who said it wasn't as bad as people make out. Ignorance is a terrible barrier to hide behind. We *can* actually find out what is happening.

The border

A little while back I was watching a fascinating Channel 4 documentary about Tex-Mex music, music that comes from the border between Texas and Mexico. It is one of my favourite musical styles, and was first brought to my attention by Ry Cooder when he toured in London a few years ago with perhaps the most famous Tex-Mex musician, Flaco Jiminez, and his band. But Tex-Mex music is not just a fusion of two creative styles of music from two different ways of life. It is music that straddles a most significant border, a border that Ry Cooder has sung about in two of his songs, 'Borderline' and 'Across the Border'. This border is the Rio Grande, or Rio Bravo as the Mexicans call it. It is the dividing line between the first world and the Third World. As the TV documentary put it, 'This is where the Third World starts.' And so yearly thousands of Mexicans struggle to cross over the Rio Grande to reach the promised land of materialism that billboard and TV adverts have taught them exists only a little way away. Thousands are prepared to make the trip at great cost to themselves every year. Heavily pregnant women travel over in order to try and have their child born in the United States, while the border police patrol the Rio Grande, stopping people and turning them back whenever they can.

The labour from south of the border has been needed, used and exploited to the full as cheap labour over the years. But once the labourers have served their purpose, they have no part in the first world – a theme taken up very well in the Woody Guthrie song, 'Plane Crash at Los Gatos' – a song which highlights the issue of people being used and then forgotten or ignored as people with no names and no significance:

> The skyplane caught fire over Los Gatos Canyon
> The fireball of lightning it struck all our hills
> Who were these friends who were scattered like dry leaves
> The radio said they were 'just deportees'
>
> ('Plane Crash at Los Gatos' – W. Guthrie,
> Tro-Essex Music Ltd)

The imagery of a river separating the North from the South, the rich from the poor, is one that sticks firmly in my mind. The borderline that divides does not only exist at the Rio Grande. It doesn't only exist in South Africa. It exists all over the world, and many times not so obviously.

When I was on the visit to South Africa, I had Ry Cooder's song 'Across the Border' with me, and it struck me how relevant it was to the situation there, because South Africa is a microcosm of the world. In fact, the country is a parable for the world. It is always easy to point the finger at South Africa, which is clearly an immoral regime, and it becomes easy to wax eloquent about injustices that are a long way away from home. But in South Africa we find in one country lessons about how the rich live off the poor, how the North treats the South, because South Africa is a rich first world country with a Third World country within its very borders.

In the UK it is relatively easy to ignore the barriers in our world because the poor seem a long way away. (We even manage to ignore the problems of our own urban inner city areas if we live outside them.) In South Africa the problem is literally down the road and the border is man-made and man-defined. The story is the same, however. People can cross the border because their labour is needed, but as soon as the work is done they have to go back to their allotted place – 'The rich man in his castle, the poor man at his gate.'

When I spoke to that group of students at Witwatersrand University, I sang for the first time a song that I'd just written, 'Nero's Watching Video':

Nero's watching video while Rome begins to burn
Nero's wearing roller skates so he can quickly turn
Get away from what he doesn't want to see or want to hear
Nero's wearing headphones and they stretch from ear to ear
Nero's got a private world for which the heart may yearn
Nero's watching video while Rome begins to burn

Ignorance is very often bliss. We actually enjoy what keeps us away from the realities that surround us. But the God of the Bible is the constantly loving God who brings us up short and reminds us to live in reality and act in reality. The borderline doesn't simply start at the Rio Grande or at Soweto, it starts in my mind and your mind. It gets reinforced if we never challenge the status quo. It gets reinforced if we never ask questions about what God really requires of us. It gets reinforced if we manage to spiritualise our faith in such a way that it has no practical application.

Zachariah the Zulu

One of the most enjoyable parts of this visit to South Africa was a trip up to the north part of Kwazulu to Manguzi Hospital which was not far from the border with Mozambique. We visited a project called 'Ngezandla Zetha' which is a Zulu phrase meaning 'with our hands'. It was a handicraft project supporting literally thousands of families. They would make the products and bring them into the hospital, then they would be distributed and sold around the country. This project was giving work and support to thousands at a time when drought had destroyed the current harvest. We saw it burnt dry in the fields. Without the project many more would have died.

Here I met a blind man called Zachariah. His life was a parable of human dignity. When he arrived at the project he had a profound effect on the other blind workers. He gave them a sense of pride and refused to let them be pitied or patronised. He was also a musician and a songwriter. Someone told me he was the 'chronicler of his people' in a place where history was not written down.

He sang me several songs – one was about the arrival of

57

cholera in his village a year or so earlier, which killed many of his friends. Another was about the 'Inquevuma incident'. This area was known as Inquevuma and the South African government made an agreement with Swaziland to give it away. Zachariah told me how his people were going to fight to keep their land and then their chief – Mangosutu Buthelezi – came and told them not to fight, and he then took the South African government to court and won. Zachariah celebrated this victory of his chief in a song.

Zachariah's faith and dignity shone out and inspired me to write a song about him – because as I said to one of my companions, 'The image of God shone brightly today'.

Zachariah the Zulu

What a terrible day when the cholera came
Mbangweni village was never the same
Took away his friends, took 'em one by one
And he tells you all about it in the words of a song.

> Zachariah sings songs, songs for his people
> He captures their spirit, their hopes and their fears
> Zachariah paints pictures that are all in the mind
> He's the eyes of his people, this man born blind.

What a sad sad day when the Government came
This land of Inquevuma they said we're giving it away
To a Northern kingdom for reasons of our own
This land that the Tonga and the Zulu call home.

> Zachariah sings songs, songs for his people . . .

Then the Chief Buthelezi came and said don't fight
I'll take up your cause, I'll pursue what is right
And Zachariah thanks God for the power of his chief
For the battle that he won and for the sense of relief.

> Zachariah sings songs, songs for his people . . .

Zachariah is proud he say now don't pity me
He say now don't say shame because I can't see
And Zachariah thanks God for the gift of a song
And for the strength that He gives to help him carry on.

> Zachariah sings songs, songs for his people . . .

© David Paramor Publishing

Graaf-Reniet

I visited another township, miles from Soweto, in a place called Graaf-Reniet, where Tear Fund was involved with a feeding programme. There was one tap for every two or three streets. There was no electricity, children were undernourished and there was appalling dust, dirt and lack of sanitation. It seemed almost unbelievable because literally across the road, within view, the richest area of that town started; a town, interestingly enough, which prides itself on being religious. In the township I met Grace – a devout Christian woman whose whole life spoke of love – who was committed to bringing hope and help to so many people in that situation. She was involved with children through her organising of feeding programmes, and with the whole community in her work as a social worker. After I met her, I discovered that her husband had been tortured by the security forces and was permanently handicapped as a result.

After coming back from this trip, I had many people come up to me and say, 'I hear that a great spiritual revival is happening in South Africa.' True, there are churches that are full, and new churches are springing up, but in what sense is it a revival? How do we actually recognise spiritual revival? If it were a revival of obedience to God, then there would be an overwhelming surge of justice and righteousness. The immorality of that warped theology of apartheid would not be tolerated. Apartheid is clearly a heresy in as far as it denies one of the basic principles of the Bible, the value of each human being as made in God's image. It dehumanises people, it separates families, it thrives on violence and injustice so that some might maintain their standard of living at the expense of others.

Yet I believe Christians hold an important key to that country as they are the ones who can offer an alternative to violence. But is it happening?

In the churches I found an overwhelming surge in the direction of personalised religion, inwards and upwards but not outwards. We see the 'me generation' reflected in religion. Churches which preach the prosperity doctrine were the fastest-growing. Fortunately that is not the whole picture, as there are many other churches that do live out the implications of the gospel. But perhaps they are not the churches that are viewed as experiencing revival.

It can be all too easy just to point the finger. I think we see the same things in European and American churches. We must be consistent in our faith. We must get rid of that borderline wherever it exists. As the prophet Micah puts it: 'The Lord has told us what is good. What he requires of us is this: to do what is just, to show constant love, and to live in humble fellowship with our God' (Micah 6:8 GNB).

Crossroads

From Graaf-Reniet I travelled on down to Cape Town, where I visited the famous Crossroads shanty town settlement. Here I met Dr Ivan Toms, who was working in the only clinic for that whole area, a clinic that has since become a focus for attention on worldwide news, and indeed has been burnt down. Ivan Toms himself has suffered arrest and imprisonment.

Here at Crossroads and then again at an area known as District Six, which had had its so-called coloured population completely removed, I began to see the results of enforced resettlement of people. I saw the terrible consequences in family and community life that this causes, and yet – in this country which is under the microscope of the world, in this country where so many churches don't seem to be living out the gospel – I came across some tremendous Christians and deep Christian faith: people who struggled for justice though there was always a price to be paid; people who prayed and worked for healing and for reconciliation in a land that is scarred and separated.

Freedom fighter

On this trip and previous trips I made friends at many different churches and saw many Christians whose stand typified the beauty and strength of a warm, vital faith committed to the removal of injustice. One church which is an example of this is St Luke's, Orchards, Johannesburg, and Peter Lee the vicar has written two books that give a valuable insight into the Bible's principles of justice to the poor and an overview of the situation in South Africa – the first is called *Poor Man, Rich Man* and the other *Guard her Children*. Much of his own experience in writing is born out of his experience of also being vicar of a church in Alexandra Township.

Fortunately there are many other examples of churches for whom spirituality is not an escape from reality, but an incentive to imitate the Incarnation and get involved in the down-to-earth issues of human poverty, deprivation and suffering.

I can well understand why Nelson Mandela and Oliver Tambo have called for certain selective violence as a response to a regime that shows constant violence. For forty years the ANC pursued peaceful means and were ignored. If we have never taken up the weapon of love and actually taken a stand against injustice, we have nothing to say to the man with the gun. He is in fact proved to be more compassionate than we are, because he has responded. I do believe there is another way, and I do believe in non-violence, but it is not the way of inactivity, for this is silent condoning of evil. I expressed my thoughts on this in a song I started writing in Ireland and finished in South Africa:

Freedom Fighter

I fear for the freedom fighter
'Cos his mind is ill at ease
He went out to fight for justice
But now he's gone and caught the disease
The cause was just and honest
But there's blood upon his hands
Women, children and good men too
And fear throughout the land.

I fear for the freedom fighter
Who chose the bloody road
Who tries to harness evil
To try to lift an evil load
And I understand the righteous wrath
That drove him to what he's done
But forgiveness lies in nail-scarred hands
Not in the hands with a gun.

I fear for a society
That always turns away
So desperate men choose desperate deeds
To try to have their say
And cold-hearted politicians
Look up in feigned surprise
As the violence is erupting
Before their very eyes.

The battle's not nearly over
It's only just begun
We write him off so easily
Say we wouldn't do what he's done
But he went 'cos he cared too deeply
For those who weep at night
There'd be no need for him to go at all
If we all did what was right.

So take up the cause of freedom
And do it with all your might
Show that the power and strength of love
Is a more powerful way to fight
And if you won't let your voice be heard
Then please don't criticise
There'd be no freedom fighters
If we weren't so compromised.

© David Paramor Publishing

There is another way. It's time to wield the weapon of love – the weapon of justice. Christians are called to be a community of hope and reconciliation who believe in a higher power. Unfortunately we have often been the silent community. We've not always supported our brothers and sisters in South Africa who struggle for justice. We have not taken to the streets to show what our attitude is to the evil of apartheid. Christians of all people should have been leading the demonstrations, because apartheid is based on a Christian heresy.

Of course, Christians have been leading – there is Bishop Trevor Huddleston, who is Chairman of the Anti-Apartheid Movement; there's the incredible world leadership of Archbishop Desmond Tutu, who has been acknowledged in his being awarded the Nobel Peace Prize. There are also leaders such as Dr Allan Boesak or Caesar Molebatsi, with his Youth Alive ministry in Soweto, or Michael Cassidy, with African Enterprise and the National Initiative for Reconciliation, and many, many others. But if the worldwide followers of Christ had taken up the cause and supported those brothers and sisters who have stood up and been counted on the issue of justice, then South Africa would have had to take notice.

If only Christians could be 'converted', then a change could come. Somebody said to me after hearing 'Freedom Fighter' that they thought a non-violent approach was the soft option. In fact, non-violence is never the soft option. It is only the soft option if it actually means inaction and doing nothing. But non-violence for Martin Luther King Jr was not a soft option. It is perhaps the hardest way of all.

But for many, they choose an option of total passivity. That is a denial of the gospel, because we are told to let our light shine. We have absolutely no grounds for criticising any guerrilla violence unless we are on the side of those who are committed to justice and peaceful change. Opting out is a denial of the gospel.

The work of prayer is one of the most important at a time like this. Praying and working for healing, reconciliation and change are at the heart of the gospel. South Africa represents the open wound of racism in our world, but as we pray for justice in that land the churches of our land will be made sensitive to the subtle racism that is an integral part of our own way of life, and the Holy Spirit will challenge us to changes in our own society and among our own neighbours.

In our own land, where unemployment is such a curse for so many people, it is not coincidental that it is highest among black and Asian young people, proportionately far higher than among white young people. When violence erupts in our own inner cities, it is not enough to cry for stronger law and order, we have to do something to deal with the injustice that lies at the very heart of the outburst in a country where the have-nots feel as if they have even less, while the haves still seem to be able to raise their standard of living despite various economic crises.

Jesus never called us to a comfortable life, he called us to take up our cross daily, he called us to be servants, to follow the road of obedience. It should never be some pious, easy spirituality that warms our own hearts while neglecting to deal with the real problems that face the society in which we live.

The borderlines need to be broken down within our own minds and within our own societies, and the body of Christ should be the community which *par excellence* shows the eradication of these barriers that divide society, because in Christ 'there is neither Jew nor Greek, slave nor free, male nor female, for you are all one in Christ Jesus' (Galatians 3:28). It's time to pray and it's time to act. As Allan Boesak says,

If the rulers will not hear the cries of the people, if they will not change, if they continue to prevent justice, let us pray them out of existence. God will hear our cry . . . We do not believe in the power of violence, but we do believe in the power of prayer. (Allan A. Boesak, SACC National Conference, June 1984)

THE SKY THAT WOULDN'T WEEP

Waiting for the rain to fall
Waiting for the rain to fall
On a land that's burned and dry
Waiting for the sky to cry.

Oh the sky that would not weep
Oh the sky that would not weep
On a land that's parched and dry
Oh the sky that would not cry.

Let it rain Lord let it rain
Hear their cry and let it rain
Lord they're hoping and they're praying
For that sweet refreshing rain.

Oh the land is hot and dry
And the cattle Lord they die
Oh shake the sky and break its heart
And cause the healing rain to start.

Let it rain Lord let it rain
Let your spirit rise again
Break the stony heart in two
Let our actions speak for you.

Let our lives be like the rain
Bringing healing in your name
Break our hearts forgive our fears
And in your mercy grant us tears.

Let it rain Lord let it rain
Let your spirit rise again
Forgive our days of 'Couldn't care'
Forgive the hand that will not share.

Oh the sky that would not weep
Oh the sky that would not weep
Break the heart – give a new beat
To the sky that would not weep
To the soul that cannot weep.

5. THE SKY THAT WOULDN'T WEEP – Kenya

'We must take what Jesus did in first-century Palestine as a series of pointers to what he is doing amongst us – and that is what God has always been doing since Moses led the Israelites out of Egypt – freeing men and women from every form of slavery, political as well as spiritual.'

President Kenneth Kaunda of Zambia

'You cannot develop people – you must allow people to develop themselves.'

President Nyerere of Tanzania

'The Spirit of the Lord is upon me, because he has chosen me to bring good news to the poor. He has sent me to proclaim liberty to the captives and recovery of sight to the blind; to set free the oppressed and announce that the time has come when the Lord will save his people.'

Luke 4:18–19 (GNB)

I had the uncanny feeling that I had just stepped back in time. Leaving the film-crew at the Land-Rover getting their equipment ready, I had walked around an outcrop of rock and arrived at the only watering hole in miles. It was an overpowering sight, a vast sandy arena where, at one end, I could make out the dull glint of thick, dirty, brown water. All around the edge were camels and goats drinking thirstily. I was astonished to spot, kneeling at the edge, hands cupped to scoop out the water, a young man dressed in skins and carrying a bow and arrow. Nearby a young goatherd was leading a straggling group of goats towards the water. There was an almost Old Testament biblical feel to the whole environment. I felt as if I had stepped through some Narnian wardrobe into a different time and place. It was a breathtaking experience.

It was March 1985 and I was in Kenya at a place called Nginyang, which was the site of a project run by the Church of the Province of Kenya. On this particular day I was with Peter Amoll, who was the Project Manager, and he was showing me the only water-pan in the area. Despite the sense of timelessness that I had on first glimpsing the water-pan, Peter pointed out to me that it had only recently been dug. This area was deeply affected by the drought – so much so that people had been abandoning their villages in the desperate search for water. The arrival of the water-pan gave a new lease of life to the area, and many had returned home as a result of it.

We interviewed some of the women who came striding gracefully and purposefully towards the water-pan with their pots balanced on their heads. Working through the local chief as our interpreter, we discovered that many of the women were walking up to ten kilometres a day to get their water. Then they faced the same ten-kilometre hike back home with the full pot of water, and this was repeated each day in order to survive. The water was, in fact, filthy, and being used by animals and humans alike. It meant that it was a breeding ground for disease. Peter explained to us that one of the priority projects they were currently working on was a scheme to make a separate area for the local people to draw their drinking water, away from where the cattle were using and polluting it.

The price of a cup of water

Peter and the chief talked sadly of the effects of drought in the area. Only two days before, they told me, a man from another district had been walking through the Nginyang area, some kilometres from the water-pan, and had asked for a cup of water. In fact he had offered the substantial Kenyan sum of fifteen shillings for a single cup. But his money was worthless in a situation where there simply was no water to give or sell.

The people left him – as they thought – sleeping. Later that same afternoon they came back to where the man was, and found that, far from being asleep as they had assumed, he had in fact died.

As Peter was driving me back to the project he pointed out to me the spot where the man had died. The red garment he had worn still hung on a branch – a lonely and tragic symbol of the high cost of a cup of water.

The Pokot

Nginyang is about forty-five minutes' drive from Lake Baringo, and the people of the area are the Pokot. To look at they are not dissimilar from the Maasai; like the Maasai they are pastoral people, and so live entirely off their cattle and livestock. Their main diet is a blend of milk and cows' blood, seasoned with a little cow urine, according to taste! Unpleasant as this may sound to us, it is in fact their main diet. Sadly, fifty percent of their livestock and cattle had already died. The rest had to be moved to wherever there were water-holes left, which could be vast distances away. Since they had lost their livelihood, people were totally dependent on the famine-relief food that was coming into the area.

The Nginyang project was a village polytechnic where skills were being taught to help people combat the tragedy that faced them. It is vitally important to get people off emergency relief as quickly as possible, and back to providing for their own needs. The drought was forcing a very deep change of life on the Pokot – having always been pastoral people, it was now necessary for them to learn basic agricultural skills since so many of their cattle were dead. Other vocational skills were being taught at the polytechnic, such as carpentry, sewing, needlework and building, in order to provide much-needed work.

Chepkoi

The polytechnic was also providing a 'food for work' building project. The work was done by the women, and having done it they would collect their food, put it on their heads, and start for home. We decided to follow one of the women and find out her story. It proved a long trek, and despite taking the Land-Rover some of the distance to carry our equipment, we still had to walk a mile or two when we were forced by the terrain to leave it.

We discovered that the woman's name was Chepkoi, and she had been married only one year. She worked at the polytechnic to provide food for her mother and grand-parents, while her husband had had to leave home to look for work. Chepkoi gave us an insight into her way of life. After she showed us how she prepared the food she had been given, she took us on her daily trip to get water. In her case it was a two-mile walk to a nearby river, where the water was now reduced to a little dirty brown trickle.

The snake hunt

Talking with Chepkoi produced one of the most entertaining and spontaneous moments of the trip – nevertheless a reminder of some of the real dangers that are faced each day. We were doing our interview for the video camera when yelling came from the nearest hut – maybe a quarter of a mile away. Someone came rushing up, calling out to Chepkoi. She began to reply, laughing as she did so. Then there was a rush of activity. Peter Amoll translated for us, and explained that there was a dangerous snake caught in the roof of her neighbour's hut.

'We must film this,' said John Muggleton, our camera-man, so we followed Chepkoi at a run. Arriving at the hut, we found Chepkoi and her neighbour armed with spears taking up positions at either side of the hut. Then Peter went very, very cautiously into the front entrance, also armed with a spear. John told me to get in close and look in the hut and give a running commentary. It was nearly a disastrous move, as Peter's spear had a sharp point at both ends, and as I edged closer there was a sudden outburst of intense jabbing activity with Peter's spear swinging back and forth in a lethal fashion. I decided to do my running commentary from another vantage point!

Eventually the wounded snake fled from the hut, and it was Chepkoi who dealt the final blow. The whole incident had been accompanied by laughter and screams, and after the kill there was much relief and celebration, and then we wandered back to try and pick up our interrupted interview.

The heartbeat of Africa

Despite the problems of the drought, the day in Chepkoi's village was a helpful experience in understanding a little more of the African way of life. Africa has been portrayed in recent years as simply a place of famine, poverty or war, and our image is often dominated by pity or by old colonial viewpoints.

Yet Africa is intriguing, both in its beauty and in the character of its way of life, and it is in the village that you come close to its heart. James Oporia-Ekworo, a Kenyan diplomat, put it this way on the recent Channel Four documentary *Consuming Hunger*. When sitting in a Kenyan village, he said:

> The village captures the story of Africa; it will never make it to the news headlines, but this is the heartbeat of Africa. This is the economic base of Africa. This is where political power eventually lies. This is the cultural repository of our people. The image that you have in the West about Africa is very different. It is the Africa of so-called barbarism: the Tarzan image of Africa on the one hand; on the other, of Africa perpetually starving, perpetually stretching out its hand to the West begging for food – without dignity, without responsibility, without self-determination.

71

James Oporia-Ekworo went on to point out that this is a false image. One has only to spend time in a village to glimpse the true Africa which has very real dignity and responsibility, and deep pride in its culture. The simplicity of its lifestyle and the strength of community relationships are areas in which we need to learn as we labour under the oppression of materialism and fragmented relationships. I spent time in the village visiting people with the local vicar. It was a valuable insight into a way of life that I will always treasure. The vicar's own concern and compassion for his people, and his desire for his people's wellbeing on every level was in itself a reminder of the wholeness and relevance of the gospel.

Waiting for the rain

As we spent the few days at Nginyang wandering around, meeting people and seeing what they were doing, we had this strange sense of everybody simply waiting. It was the time when the rains should have started. Planting had been done, and now there was nothing else to do but wait and hope and pray for the rain to fall. One of my strongest memories of Nginyang is that of the barren windswept soil. The wind was sweeping the topsoil away, and even when the rains do come, they come so suddenly and with such force that they, too, sweep the topsoil away into the river. At one point I walked for some distance down a huge barren gully which led into the river, a vast dried-up river bed where a woman was digging a hole to try and get some water – she had in fact dug about ten or twelve feet in order to get it. In a short period of time, with an African storm, that dried-up river bed could become a raging torrent.

Surprisingly, Africa's rainfall is not that low, but because of the fierce unpredictability of its coming, the major problem is storing it for the future. Apart from drought periods, the normal rainfall is ample, but it comes so suddenly that it cannot be captured, and often takes the topsoil away with it in the ferocity of its onslaught.

After walking around at Nginyang, I wrote the song,

'The Sky That Wouldn't Weep' – a sort of blues for the situation there, of people waiting for the rain to come. We were making a video for Tear Fund, and that evening we looked at the material we had shot during the day. There was that same extraordinary mood captured even on video of the sense of expectancy – of almost a hush over every-thing as people waited for those first sweet refreshing drops of rain to fall.

> Waiting for the rain to fall
> Waiting for the rain to fall
> On a land that's burned and dry
> Waiting for the sky to cry . . .
>
> Let it rain Lord let it rain
> Hear their cry and let it rain
> Lord they're hoping and they're praying
> For that sweet refreshing rain.
>
> Oh the land is hot and dry
> And the cattle Lord they die
> Oh shake the sky and break its heart
> And cause the healing rain to start.

Then the song becomes a parable, looking back at our own society, where we too have a drought, but this time not a drought of rain, but a drought of spiritual and community life.

In my visits to the so-called Third World, every time I have found that I have been enriched. Too often we put a spotlight only on their poverty, which is a material poverty, but often in terms of spirituality and their communities they are very rich and have much to teach us in areas where we are all too often so bankrupt. We have a responsibility to be just in our dealing with the Third World and to share with them in their need, yet strangely it will be in our doing justice and in our giving, that we receive and capture some of the things our society has lost.

> Let it rain Lord let it rain
> Let your Spirit rise again
> Break the stony heart in two
> Let our actions speak for you.

Let our lives be like the rain
Bringing healing in your name
Break our hearts forgive our fears
And in your mercy grant us tears.

Let it rain Lord let it rain
Let your Spirit rise again
Forgive our days of 'Couldn't care'
Forgive the hand that will not share.

The vicar and the local chief at Nginyang invited me to do a concert at the church. It was a lovely occasion – the chief had just finished organising a food distribution, and before going home everyone crowded into the church for an impromptu and informal concert. Their response was heart-warming, and when I started to introduce 'Namirembe' (see chapter two) my translator turned to me in absolute delight, and pointed out that she was Ugandan and had worked for years at Mengo Hospital on Namirembe hill.

Ending these concerts is always difficult when there is such enthusiasm, but the problem was solved on this occasion by the arrival of an unbelievable sandstorm that drowned out the possibility of any more singing and sent our film crew desperately scurrying to cover all the equipment. Though it was something the Pokot were well used to, I sensed their excitement that maybe the rain wasn't too far away. We also felt that excitement when, before we finally left Nginyang, there were those first few precious drops of rain that would mean so much in that barren and windswept area.

Kodich

From Nginyang we embarked on a spectacular drive, crossing the Cherangani Hills and going through the Kerio Valley, where the East African Safari Rally takes place. The drivers were already practising for the rally, and we became aware of the havoc these sorts of events cause to the local inhabitants, since the drivers are driving on roads where there is no fencing and through villages, causing danger to both humans and livestock alike.

From here we headed up to a place called Kodich. We were fairly close to Mount Elgin, which straddles the border between Uganda and Kenya – indeed this part of Kenya had been part of Uganda some years back. That night I did another impromptu concert – this time by hurricane lamp – in the local church. It was another exuberant occasion. With the choir of the church, they sang songs to welcome us, and I sang songs back to them. Then at the end everybody left the church, all dancing to a song, and lined up outside. We had to go out and shake hands with each one of them. When we got to the end of the line, it all seemed to start again, with everyone shaking hands with everyone else, all moving to the rhythm of a song of praise. It was one of those occasions when you pinch yourself and wonder, 'Am I really here?' What a privilege to enter for a moment into the lives of people who are so different and yet with whom we have such unity because of our mutual love for Jesus Christ.

But life here was not easy. Water was just as hard to come by in this area, and again we saw the daily struggle to combat the effects of the drought, a drought that here also was destroying the natural way of life, and therefore new jobs and agricultural skills had to be taught to enable people to survive.

Here we met Richard Suffern, a Tear Fund worker who was helping at the local village polytechnic, a project of the Church of the Province of Kenya. He explained that a well had been put in recently because of a cholera epidemic. Before that, people had dug for water by hand (as we had just seen them doing at Nginyang) on a dry river bed. Then they had to get in with their feet because of digging so deep for the water, but of course the water was made dirty, and so disease was spread.

Ndeiya

It was now time for me to head home, so I left our film crew still filming in the Kodich area, and I headed back with Tear Fund's East African representatives, John and Jenny Lawford, on the long journey from Kodich to Nairobi.

75

Reminiscing over the previous couple of weeks, I realised that the trip to Kenya had surprised me. It is a country which I assumed was one of those best able to cope with this crisis. It is economically better off than many other African countries, so I hadn't been prepared for how deeply the crisis had bitten into its very heart. On my first day I had travelled only about thirty kilometres from Nairobi to a place near Limuru called Ndeiya. This is one of the main food-growing areas of Kenya, and yet right here we found Tear Fund and several other agencies involved in a famine-relief programme.

The project at Ndeiya is called Guthairira, and there were many different aspects of work going on here. On my second morning, I remember visiting some of the agricultural work, and standing on a field and seeing the topsoil being blown off in the fierce winds that raged around this particular district. It made me aware of the nature of the battle that they faced, and as I saw the enthusiasm of the workers, it gave me an understanding of the commitment with which it was being fought. At every project we visited, we saw not only the vast problems, but also the struggle for a future – the signs of hope. As I put it in a verse for a song for the *Candle in the Darkness* video:

> On the Northern plains of Kenya
> Upon the dusty land
> We saw the battle raging
> As each one took their stand
> In hands that worked the soil
> In hands that worked the wood
> In hands that build a future
> In hands that work for good

Everywhere we went, people were working and fighting against the overwhelming odds. It was a deeply hopeful sign among the problems to see the digging, the planting, and the people learning new skills that would provide new work. The battle for a future beyond the immediate crisis had been joined.

Heading home

The journey from Kodich to Nairobi, along the Great Rift Valley, reminded me again of the majestic beauty of Africa. *En route* we passed Lake Nakuru, famous as the home of the world's greatest concentration of flamingoes who gather there to feed on its soda-rich water and in turn give it that extraordinary pink hue that makes it so distinctive. Though it still looked decidedly pink to me, I was told that the water level had never been so low, and that the quantity of flamingoes was considerably reduced.

At Nakuru there was yet another reminder of the people's predicament, as we learnt that Lake Nakuru Game Reserve, which borders the lake, was being invaded by more and more of the local people on a desperate mission for food and water. For those who are so passionately concerned about wildlife, as I believe we should be, there is a need to recognise that this cannot be preserved at the expense of human beings, for the two are inextricably interwoven. If we want the wildlife to survive, then first we have to do something about the human population who are in such desperate need.

As Lloyd Timberlake points out in *Africa in Crisis*:

Africa's hundreds of national parks and game reserves have been established and run with almost all their attention on animals and tourism, and almost no attention on local Africans. The system has never worked particularly well, and pressures upon it are growing. 'The idea of "national parks" as it is presently conceived is an alien and unacceptable idea to the African population', according to Kenyan ecologist Walter Lusigi. 'It is one thing to keep urban Americans from farming Yellowstone, quite another to keep the Maasai herders out of Kenya's Amboseli Reserve.'

Africa is fighting for survival against the terrible enemy of creeping desert which is moving relentlessly further south year by year. There are ways of fighting the desert and providing long-term solutions, but all of us need the will, because the resources that are needed are so huge. There may be those who think they have done their bit for Africa – in fact the battle has only just begun.

> Let our lives be like the rain
> Bringing healing in your name
> Break our hearts forgive our fears
> And in your mercy grant us tears.
>
> Let it rain Lord let it rain
> Let your Spirit rise again
> Forgive our days of 'Couldn't care'
> Forgive the hand that will not share.
>
> Oh the sky that would not weep
> Oh the sky that would not weep
> Break the heart – give a new beat
> To the sky that would not weep
> To the soul that cannot weep.

A WORLD OF DIFFERENCE

A world of difference, a world of need
one dies of hunger, one dies of greed
a world of wonder, a world of pain
the gifts we're given get used in vain.

    We have the power to make or break
    we have the power to wheel and deal
    we have the power to give or to take
    we have the power to heal or steal.

A world of laughter, a world of tears
each new day breaking brings untold fears
a world of beauty, a world to share
but who believes that, who can hear?

    We have the skill to heal the ill
    we have the skill to right the wrong
    we have the skill to restore or to kill
    we have the skill to make weak the strong.

A world of difference . . . a world of need
a world of beauty . . . a world of greed.

6. A WORLD OF DIFFERENCE – Sudan

'Because we cannot see Christ we cannot express our love to him; but our neighbours we can see, and we can do to them what if we saw him, we should like to do to Christ.'

Mother Teresa of Calcutta

'Man is God's image; but a poor man is Christ's stamp to boot.'

George Herbert

'Must the hunger become anger and the anger fury before anything will be done?'

John Steinbeck

It was 13 July 1985. We were listening to the BBC World Service as we came over the brow of a slight hill, and there in front of us was the sadly all-too-familiar sight of thousands upon thousands of brown low-slung tents that came to form the image of refugee camps in the eyes of the world. As we caught our first glimpse of the refugee camp, the World Service announced the start of 'Live Aid' in Wembley, London. It was a curious moment: it gave us a sense of unity of purpose. For a moment the world put aside its endless pursuit of evil and greed, and seemed to link arms to do something about some of the injustice and suffering. We were, at that moment, somehow at the sharp point of what had made 'Live Aid' necessary. Our brief from Tear Fund, who were sponsoring this trip, was to investigate the refugee situation, to see the reality of the famine and drought; to see what was being done, and to see the possibilities of what could be done. We were also making a video of the trip.

Shagarab One

The camp we were now driving into was known as Shagarab One, or Shagarab East, a refugee reception camp of about ten thousand Eritreans. There were three Shagarab camps. Shagarab Two also held around ten thousand, largely Tigreans, and we were only to catch a frustratingly small glimpse of that camp, for the most surprising of reasons. Shagarab Three had another four thousand people. Eritrean camps were distinguished by the flags they had flying above their tents, which were predominantly red and seemed to be different designs, according to the area they came from in Eritrea. It was an image that implanted itself so strongly in our minds that when we came to do an autumn-to-Christmas presentation for Tear Fund, called *A Candle in the Darkness*, we made the stage resemble a refugee tent, complete with a red flag flying, and the presentation started off with sounds recorded in Shagarab One.

Caught in a demonstration

This camp was a well-organised one, and we were shown around by Kamal Tag Elsir, the manager of the camp, who worked for the Sudan Commission on Refugees. Though it was well-organised, we were soon to discover that all these camps were desperately short of much-needed resources.

Because we had a video camera with us, we were soon caught up in a demonstration. It seemed that some of the refugees saw the opportunity to make a protest in front of what they took to be a TV camera. I found myself in a quite bizarre situation, as hundreds of people crowded around us and showed us the food that they were given each day. They were pointing out how it was inadequate, and that the flour was completely the wrong sort of flour for their diet as they were unable to make their normal bread with it.

Since we had the head of the camp there, and their protest was in a sense aimed at me, I felt I had to take some sort of intermediary role, and so put to him the questions that were being asked by the people. He accepted their complaints and said he knew it was the wrong flour, but they had been sent the wrong flour and they simply had no other resources at all – they had run out of money. This hopelessly inadequate diet was nevertheless the only diet for the people living in this camp.

The demonstration was amazingly good-natured, although it did seem particularly tense at first as the people crowded in on us, but when they heard Kamal Tag's reply, they felt that their protest had been registered, so they broke up with smiles and shook hands, content that their point had been made. They then spent their time welcoming us and showing us the various ways they were trying to make life better in the camp.

'Have you got a job for me?'

Perhaps one of the biggest surprises I was to get was how many times I was asked the question, 'Have you got a job for me?' It seemed somehow a surprising echo of home. Often we assume that if we feed people who are starving, then all is done; we forget that the very style of diet is important, and then there's health, sanitation, but beyond all that, if you have ten thousand people sitting in a field, what are they actually going to do? The need for vocational job training and for the creation of job skills and job schemes was paramount in this camp as it was in every camp we visited.

Sanitation

Sanitation was another major problem. The Red Cross nurse who showed us around, Elizabeth Lamb, pointed out a field, and said, 'Come down here at five o'clock and you'll find thousands of people all defecating at one time.' I asked incredulously, 'You mean there's no proper sanitation in the camp?' She said, 'None at all.' Naturally, this situation makes it very hard to control disease, and in fact there'd been a recent outbreak of cholera in that camp, an outbreak that had miraculously been contained without the loss of life, but nevertheless the danger was obvious. Elizabeth Lamb and the other workers that we met in the camp were doing a great work, labouring away against the odds.

Elizabeth took us to the little hospital where they were trying to organise feeding programmes for those who were particularly showing signs of malnutrition. Here I saw a tragically thin three-year-old girl called Halima, who was just skin and bones. I was surprised to discover that Halima had been on an emergency feeding programme for three months and yet was still so extraordinarily thin. She had the most beautiful smile on her face and had obviously benefited enormously from this feeding programme – but it made me realise just what sort of a condition she must have been in three months before.

Then came the rain

At the end of this day in Shagarab One, we briefly went off to visit Shagarab Two, with the intention of filming there the next day. With curious irony, in this time of drought, it was rain that prevented us from getting there. During the night it poured with rain. We set out the next morning with the nurses from Christian Outreach who were working in Shagarab Two. We were a small convoy of vehicles trying to get through – a jeep from Medicins sans Frontières, and one or two other workers from different agencies – but that morning nobody made it. When it rains the ground in that part of the Sudan turns completely to mud. We got bogged down, and though we got out and pushed in mud that went up to our knees and beyond, in the end we had to try and pull one another out and head back.

It accentuated one of the problems of the camps in that area, which was that if the rainy season properly came, those camps were cut off, and even flooded. At Shagarab

One people told us how they'd been flooded, and how they had had to stand there holding their children because the water was up to the waists of the adults. Apart from the discomfort, the disease problems are obviously magnified by such a situation. It was the sheer size and scale of the disaster, and the difficulty of some of the practical dimensions of bringing help and of dealing with it, that were hard for people to grasp if they just observed some of the news bulletins.

Long-term refugees

As we were heading back from our abortive attempt to reach Shagarab Two, we were met by Omer Saad Abdel Hameed, of the Sudan Commission on Refugees, who was project manager for the Eastern region of Sudan. He had suspected that we wouldn't get through, and he asked us to come and see another camp which was in the town of Khasm-el-Gherba. This was a camp of Ethiopian refugees that had been there since 1978. I had not been aware that refugees had been coming across from Eritrea for that long, and it meant that already there had been a refugee camp for seven years.

Again the biggest question in the camp was, 'Have you got a job for me?' and again I was constantly reminded of the dignity and the necessity of work. The camp had built its own schools, had its own churches and mosque, and had become what indeed it was, a mini-town of ten thousand people, but it was not a problem that would go away, as most of these refugees were unable or unwilling to return. Hence they needed some means of livelihood – yet their very presence was a threat to the local community, which itself lived very close to the breadline and whose jobs were all too few, even prior to the arrival of the refugees.

An attack of dysentery

We were filming all morning in this camp and it was a very warm day. As it was getting hotter towards midday, our sound man, Peter Novell, was gradually beginning to keel over with dysentery, which first struck him and then hit David Bainbridge, our guide. It necessitated taking a day's pause as these two were looked after by the nurses at the Christian Outreach compound. We couldn't afford any longer time than one day as we knew we had to move on the next day to visit some other camps.

Unfortunately, during that night I also developed dysentery, and I will never forget the drive across from Khasm-el-Gherba to a town called Wad Menani. The three of us were in a dreadful state. There's nothing more crippling to one's pride than to be uncontrollably going from both ends at once! As our Hiace van trundled across the dusty terrain, periodically it would stop and three figures would emerge on the run, darting for some semblance of a bush, to re-emerge a little while later, and to climb back into the van, much slower than their exit had been.

I reached my worst on the outskirts of Wad Menani, and we were due that night to be pressing on to a place called Senna, where we had heard that there was a Chadian refugee camp which had only recently been set up and was badly in need of support. The Fellowship for African Relief, whom David and Magdy Makrum – our other guide – were working for, were keen to be involved at that camp, and so we wanted to go and assess the need in the hope that something more could be done. En route we went to a hotel to take a brief stop, where I more or less collapsed.

Eventually they all came back and woke me up. I realised they'd let me sleep for longer than I had expected, and I began slowly to get out of bed, only to be told that instead of resuming our journey to Senna we were simply moving to another hotel. They had decided to give me a night in a good bed to try and recover, and the next day we would complete the last stretch of our trip. It was a great relief to spend a night in a hotel, in a room that even had a shower, and although it wasn't exactly a restful night, at least it gave me the strength to go on and face what would perhaps be one of the most harrowing days of our time in Sudan.

Chadian camp

We travelled down to Senna, and arrived at the Chadian camp. Once there we discovered that the refugees had travelled over a thousand miles to be in that area. They had travelled so far because it is where the railway ends and they had hitched a ride on the train. There was in fact virtually no food in between at all. They were fleeing from war and from famine, and in talking with some of the people, with an interpreter, I asked them if they would go back. All of those I asked simply said no; and I said, 'What happens when the famine is over?' They seemed to have a very depressed view, and just said, 'The famine won't be over, we'll never go back.'

We arrived to find an extraordinary situation: there were a couple of workers from Bristol, Don and Nicola Alexander, who were being supported by World Vision, and they had set up the only feeding programme in the camp, which was feeding about three hundred children. The strange part was that their practical support for handing out the food was coming from the Muslim Brotherhood, who at the time we arrived had just gone off duty to have their breakfast, leaving women and children standing in the blazing sun in a dreadful condition. Don and Nicola, who were in the process of grappling with the frustration of this, were delighted to see us and were obviously keen that others would get involved in the work of the camp.

There seemed to be virtually no food around at all for adults, and a quarter of the children had died in the month prior to our arrival. In fact there was a makeshift clinic which, Don explained to me, had been full at the beginning of the week. I was slightly confused as to why it was no longer full, and wondered if this indicated that people were getting better. They weren't. Tragically, as Don said, 'The clinic is a death cell; people don't come out of it alive.' They had all died during that week.

It was a clinic of the most rudimentary nature. They had none of the proper medical facilities at all, and one of the saddest sounds I'll always remember is leaving the camp and hearing babies start to cry from the clinic again, and knowing that they were in a sense sentenced to death by the mere fact that they were so ill that they had to be brought into such a place. As we drove out with heavy clouds all around us, a thunderstorm was about to break over the camp – it was to the chorus of those pitiful cries.

It had been a difficult day's filming in the camp, partly because both I and our sound man, Peter, were ill, and also because it was a camp that was in the worst condition of any that we saw. We had looked first at the feeding programme, and some basic hygiene methods that were being shown to people, then we had walked around talking to people, interviewing them, and filming.

In a strange way, my own dysentery helped to bring home to me the tremendous need of that situation. I knew that I could leave the camp and get treatment – even in the Sudan; and if that wasn't good enough I could fly home and get the best treatment that is available – yet there were people who were dying of acute cases of dysentery in the camps. What's more, for many of them, they have known of no existence apart from the dysentery of some sort that's accompanied them all their lives. Somehow for a moment it gave me a brief insight into the reality of life – a life that I could walk away from, but a life that others have to live with, and, of course, from which they also die.

A child is the future

Despite the poverty and tragedy of that camp, I remember some very cheerful moments. The children in particular stick vividly in my mind. They had made little makeshift toys out of whatever was available, and though they had the obvious signs of malnutrition – swollen bellies, hair changing colour because of lack of vitamins – as they played together I was reminded again of the incredible worth of every human being. There was that spark of life that reminded me of the image of God which is in each one of us.

I thought of a song that I had recorded a couple of months before, called 'A Child is the Future', and somehow that has become to me the theme song of that camp:

Oh Namirembe
Oh the hill of peace
Oh Namirembe
God's love will
   never cease

Garth with Bishop Misaeri Kauma on Namirembe Hill, Kampala.

In Haiti, singing at a school for handicapped children – 'we are tomorrow's world'.

Then I see the thirsty earth
Cracked and sandy brown
Five years of drought have done their worst
No water to be found.

(Water, water)

Drought situation in Southern India.
The last day in the villages of Southern India – the joy of striking water!

With Mother Teresa in Calcutta.
In Vankiya village, Gujerat, not long after the cyclone.

This impromptu concert was soon stopped by the train guard – en route to New Delhi.

At Guthairira, Kenya – writing down song lyrics and chords for local musicians.

This is a litany for Africa
A litany for Africa
The wound has gone so deep
God bless Africa
Guard her children
Guide her leaders
Give her peace
And Lord, make us instruments
                    of your peace.

Soweto.
Meeting children at a nursery school in Meadowland, Soweto.

The camp of Chadian refugees at Senna, in the Sudan.
Elizabeth Lamb, a Red Cross nurse, introduces Garth to Halima at Shagarab camp.

A child is tomorrow
If only she is free
From the cruel chains of poverty.

(A child of the future)

In Kenya with Tear Fund worker, John Lawford, visiting Guthairira project.
Up at the village polytechnic at Nginyang, Kenya.

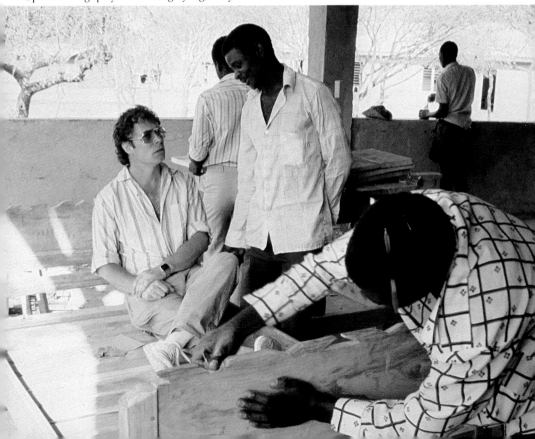

Garth in action at Greenbelt '86 – 'Light a Candle in the Darkness'.
Gill.

Abi, Tom, Ben and Joe.

All photographs © Greenleaf.

I can't wait to be with you again
Back where those loving arms will
I can't wait to be back home again
Fly me, silver wings, across the se

(Physical pain)

A child caught within a cruel world
What does the future hold?
What chance of growing old?
Her constant companions hunger and disease
Who will break the chain?
Who will heal the pain?

But a child is the future – a child is the dawn
New hope arrives when a child is born
A child is tomorrow if only she is free
From the cruel chains of poverty.

So roll back the darkness – bring on the dawn
Break the chains of poverty and blow that freedom horn
If you do it to the children – you do it unto Me
So Jesus told His followers and He tells you and me.

Those who claim that human beings do have meaning, that their lives are of significance, that there is a God who cares, have one of the biggest burdens hanging over them at the moment: to actually show our world that these are not mere words. Our concern to share the gospel of Christ cannot be left to mere words, otherwise we are not credible. Unless love is shown in actions that actually say that people matter, say that they are valued, there is no way we can introduce people to a loving Father. They must first of all see that we are such followers of this loving Father as we show his love in action.

In a world that has so much suffering and pain, in a world that's now a global village in which we know what's happening all around it, there can be no evangelism unless it is actually linked to the showing of the character of a God whose commitment is to the poor, to the oppressed, to the hungry, to the wounded, to the lonely. Any evangelism that doesn't reflect that in its attitude is actually not evangelism at all, because it has no good news for the poor; it is not setting free the oppressed – it is only adding extra security for the well-to-do, and that is not the gospel that Jesus came to proclaim.

You are never the same person after you've sat in a camp like the one at Senna. Superficial triumphalist miracle-orientated Christianity seems utterly hollow in that context. It has the hollow ring of a self-indulgent faith for those who are already far too self-indulgent, in a world where they are being strangled by materialism.

Once again I experienced the paradox that it is only in giving that we will receive the much-needed spiritual and community life for which our own society is so desperately in need. Soon after coming home from that trip I saw a photograph in the Christian press of a fleet of new cars that had been bought by a new Christian church who proclaimed that only the best would do because they are children of the King and therefore they must live like princes. How ironical, I thought; what a distortion of the true picture of Christianity! Jesus came riding on a donkey for the very purpose of rejecting that sort of wealth and power and status. He had no place to lay his head, he identified with the poor and the needy. Christianity is at the crossroads because the question is, Which side will Christians be on? Will we continue to endorse the unjust systems of our world, the inequalities, or will we take up the message that runs right through the Bible – of the compassionate heart of God for those who are in need? Ironically they have so much to offer us, if only we in turn will reach out to them.

We left the camp at Senna and travelled back to Wad Menani, where we managed to go and visit a doctor to get ourselves checked out and discovered that we had various forms of dysentery. My own was of the amoebic variety. They gave me a drug which they said would clear it up; it seemed to suit me very well, although once I got home they pointed out to me that it had been struck off the World Health list three months earlier, so I was immediately put on to a different drug which had some pretty devastating side effects on me!

On my return trip I had to take some of the film equipment with me back to the UK, and it was heavily above the baggage allowance. Having told the man from KLM what we'd been doing, he not only waived all the fees, but also bumped me up to Business Class for the trip, which was a most welcome gift in the light of my state of health.

On the flight back, my thoughts drifted back to my flight home from the previous trip, from Kenya. On that journey, I'd met up with Richard Franceys, a lecturer in technology at Loughborough University. He specialised in the area of water and waste engineering in developing countries, and I believe that on this trip he'd been out doing some work for Oxfam. He had also at previous times worked for the Church Missionary Society and also for Tear Fund.

I had pumped him for ideas, as one naturally does when one comes across a person who is an expert, and it was interesting to see the very complete view that he had of life and of the gospel. He quoted President Nyerere of Tanzania who had said, 'You can't develop people – you must allow people to develop themselves,' and pointed out that though you can supply everything in terms of health and water and education, and food and agricultural needs, one of the most important things that you must supply people with is motivation, so that in the end they can help themselves and have a fullness of life in every way. He said that this was something of which the Marxists are well aware, so they have a particular concern for people's motivation; but he said that the greatest motivation of all is the Christian one, and it is important that people are introduced to the gospel of Jesus Christ in every aspect.

On this trip I recalled our conversation and thought again of the importance of this, of the need for people to discover the tremendous motivating power of the love of Jesus Christ which shows them their value as human beings, and at the same time to be given facilities that allow them to have a level of life which is more than simply surviving, or not surviving, at the borderline of life itself. This is the message being lived out in action. The gospel is extraordinary because it is a whole message for whole people, it is not just one thing or another. Too often it has been divided up into social action or evangelism, but it loses its power immediately it is divided up. It loses its power if social action is only done as a motive for evangelism, because the true gospel has compassion at its heart, and as people see that they see the nature and character of God himself.

'Live Aid'

When I got back home from the Sudan I discovered that Gill had videoed most of 'Live Aid', and as I sat down to run through the tapes, she told me that at the end of the proceedings, after the concerts had finished in the stadiums, the television was still broadcasting from a club in London. Cliff Richard had been doing some concerts up in Birmingham and had raised some money for 'Live Aid'. He had come down and presented this to Bob Geldof, and then he'd sung a song of mine that I'd written a few years earlier, called 'A World of Difference', to finish the 'Live Aid' broadcast. As I looked at Cliff singing this on the video, I thought how well it summed up the world that I'd just returned from, and the world that I'd just moved back into:

> A world of difference, a world of need
> one dies of hunger, one dies of greed
> a world of wonder, a world of pain
> the gifts we're given get used in vain.
>
> A world of laughter, a world of tears
> each new day breaking brings untold fears
> a world of beauty, a world to share
> but who believes that, who can hear?

NO ONE IS AN ISLAND

No one is an island complete on his own
Each person's life must touch us too
So when you hear the bell toll, don't simply walk away
Remember that the bell rings out for you.

Spare a thought as you travel – for those who live in fear
For those who face the battle and the pain
No one is an island, together we stand or fall
Together we must learn to take the strain.

> To those whom much is given
> So much will be required
> A generous heart delights the heart of God.
> To those whom much is given
> So much will be required
> Loving hands reveal the mind of God.

There's only one Father, who breathed His life in all
And planted His own likeness in each one
So when you turn your eyes away, turn and look again
Remember that you're looking at God's son.

> To those whom much is given
> So much will be required
> A generous heart delights the heart of God.
> To those whom much is given
> So much will be required
> Loving hands reveal the mind of God.

7. NO ONE IS AN ISLAND – reflections on famine and relief

'We must learn this invitation of Christ: those who wish to come after me must renounce themselves. Let them renounce themselves, renounce their comforts, renounce their personal opinions, and follow only the mind of Christ, which can lead us to death but will surely also lead us to resurrection.'

Archbishop Oscar Romero

'I am convinced that often the world doesn't take us (Christians) seriously because we are so much like the world; we are caught up in the same miserable rat race of self-seeking consumerism and materialism.'

Tom Sine

'I am puzzled about which Bible people are reading when they suggest religion and politics don't mix.'

Archbishop Desmond Tutu

As I said towards the end of the last chapter, once on the plane I was able to sit back and reflect on my journey to the refugee camps in the Sudan, and as I picked up my first English newspaper for a couple of weeks I thought also about 'Live Aid'. In that paper there was a report of a parliamentary discussion, with Prime Minister Margaret Thatcher congratulating 'Live Aid' for its success and Neil Kinnock (leader of the opposition Labour Party) agreeing and saying it was 'humanity in action', but then saying:

By the same token is it not inhumanity in action when the Government cuts 18% off the aid budget in real terms in five years, when that same Government reduces the aid budget by 3% in real terms – £40 million – in this year, and despite the emergency in Sudan and Ethiopia over the last two years have not added one single penny to its aid budget except for the Hercules Service, which you are now thinking of withdrawing? 'With a record like that what price the brotherhood of man?' The only way in which the Government was prepared to provide short-term aid to the starving was by robbing the hungry of the world as it shuffled the aid budget around.

Mrs Thatcher retorted that she was proud of the Government record on aid.

Sitting in the Chadian camp had made me angry, and reading of this parliamentary debate in the *Daily Telegraph* on the plane also angered me. It is awful to have seen the sharp end of poverty and then to see such a lame reaction from one's own country. As the *Guardian* put it in a report on 21 July:

Aid statistics released by the government yesterday showed that aid from Britain last year as a proportion of the gross national product was one of the lowest in the developed world and lower than at any time in the past ten years.

The United Nations General Assembly set a target figure of at least 0·7% of GNP at the start of the second development decade in 1971.

Britain's highest recorded percentage, according to yesterday's figures from the government's statistical services was 0·52% in 1979. Last year's figure was 0·33%. Among the OECD countries, the highest proportion is recorded for Holland where the total aid was £949 million, or just over 1% of GNP. Britain comes twelfth out of seventeen countries, between Japan and Italy. Norway, Denmark and Sweden are the next highest after Holland. The United States came last with a proportion of 0·24% of GNP.

At the end of 1986, in a report by the Research Unit of Christian Aid, it was revealed that between 1979 and 1985 official development assistance fell in real terms, by twenty-nine percent. Christian Aid described the findings of the report *British Overseas Aid 1979 to 1985* as 'an insult to the world's poor'. And in 1985, while voluntary agencies, in the wake of Bob Geldof's massive campaign for famine victims, enjoyed a boom year for raising money and gave away over £130 million, British banks were actually taking back more from poor countries in interest repayments than the charities were able to give away.

Warning of famine

For two years the world had been warned of the imminent famine by Oxfam and the other relief agencies, but it was only when the television pictures first came through of Michael Buerk and Mohammed Amin's now famous report from Korem that people began to take notice. Such was the public outcry that governments at last had to respond because they saw it as a voting issue.

Up to that point, nothing had been done to avert perhaps the greatest crisis our world has known this century. It took a dishevelled pop singer to take the world by the throat and make it face up to its responsibilities to do something about this incredible tragedy that not only had been prophesied and foreseen but had been studiously ignored until people were dying in their millions.

Auschwitz – Birkenau

On a freezing cold February day earlier that same year (1985) I stood in Auschwitz and Birkenau in Poland – the Nazi concentration camps that killed the highest number of Jews in the last war. In the area of the gas ovens, a wreath with candles on it had been left by some of the surviving victims who had recently come back to visit Auschwitz. On the wreath it said, 'The world must never let this happen again.'

I stood there quietly thinking not only of the horrors of the Holocaust that are brought so close in that terrible place but also of the millions literally dying in Africa at that very moment, and I thought that the world, in a very different way, is letting it happen again. Nobody ever seems to heed the warnings of history.

A large number of our newspapers don't even carry news, they are simply gossip columns. It is of more interest to them to portray the trivial daily lives of television personalities, people who, in the words of sociologist Daniel Bell, 'are well known for being well known', than it is to report the much more boring hard facts of thousands dying of famine or of injustice around our world.

Millions were dying in Africa at the time I stood in Auschwitz, and millions are facing starvation today because of the continuation of famine or simply because so many live too close to the poverty level. For some it is because of the southern advance of the Sahara or because of a plague of locusts or because of war – all sorts of reasons.

As we look around our world the horrors of Auschwitz are still there – whether it's the four million refugees who have been forced to flee from Afghanistan because of the Russian policy of lowering the population to a manageable level; whether it's the massacres that have occurred within that country; whether it's America arming the Contras in Nicaragua and building towards another Vietnam. Vietnam in turn had the horror of an Auschwitz with its devastating bombing both in that country and of course in Cambodia too, with the avowed desire to 'bomb it back to the Stone Age'. We forget too easily.

It was unpleasant to wander around Auschwitz, to stand by the wall of death, to look at the gas ovens, to go through the pitiful sight of Birkenau on a cold snowy morning, the temperatures in the region of −23°, and to catch an echo of the haunted suffering that happened in that place. Yet perhaps it is good that it has been preserved as a museum of horror, because our memories are far too short.

Only one year after 'Live Aid' I was doing a concert in Canada, and somebody said to me, 'Garth, why do you sing so much about the issue of hunger, surely that was "last year's thing"?' – as if somehow it was OK to sing about it in 1985 because it was the fashion, but now it was not any longer. It struck me as the horrifying slavery of our obsession with fashion – if everybody is speaking and singing about hunger, then it is OK for all of us, but if it's out of fashion, forget it. But for the follower of Christ, fighting evil of all kinds remains on the agenda all the time. Fighting for justice does not go out of fashion.

We seem to have lost sight of issues of justice, of pursuing justice for its own sake, of pursuing truth for its own sake, of pursuing right living or righteousness for its own sake. It matters what newspaper we read, it matters what television programmes we watch. Far too many of us are dominated by fantasy programmes, or by newspapers that refuse to print world news in their desire for the latest gossip or titillation. Reading many of our tabloids, one comes to understand the irony of Malcolm Muggeridge when he says – with his knowing grin – of Mother Teresa, 'She never reads the newspapers, never watches the television and never listens to the radio . . . so she has a pretty good idea of what is going on in the world.'

But it cannot be left at that, because the telling of truth is a vital role for the media, as anyone who has been under any situation of state censorship will know. So we need to stop taking newspapers that deny that very name, and to start motivating the newspaper industry to give us news. We need to remind them that their responsibility is to share truth as we live in a wounded world and that we need to be shown the truth of that world so we in turn can become those with compassionate hearts with a desire for justice.

Reporting the famine

Now the news has come out about the reporting of the famine it is quite horrifying to see how long it was not reported properly because 'the story was not judged to be "big" in terms of audience appeal' (from the *Guardian* article, 'Hungry for Catastrophe', 20 October 1986). 'The inherited journalistic wisdom was that for the story to count, the disaster had to be huge and pictures had to be dramatic,' says Amin (Mohammed Amin, photographer of Michael Buerk's newspiece from Korem). 'It was the American elections, and no-one was interested in a few starving kids.'

When the story did break, according to Greg Philo in his article 'Hungry for Catastrophe',

> Many television professionals were genuinely surprised at the intense and prolonged level of public interest. Michael Buerk recalled how people from NBC said to him, 'It will only last a week; the American public will soon get bored with that sort of stuff,' and he comments how wrong they were.

Not interested in famine

It is startling to discover that even when Michael Buerk came back from Korem with those desperate scenes that he had filmed, many of the world's biggest news organisations still actually turned the story down.

Michael Buerk told Greg Philo, 'The pictures were the property of Visnews, not the BBC . . . Visnews offered the material to Eurovision on the 23rd and they rejected it, it was offered to NBC in the States on the 23rd and they rejected it.' Eventually both those agencies did run the pictures. In their book *News out of Africa*, Harrison and Palmer tell a story of how on the day of the Buerk–Amin report, the BBC offered a full set of pictures to the *Sun*. The response was, 'We are actually not interested in famine.' Five days later, when the story had broken, the *Sun* ran two-inch headlines: 'Race to save the babies.'

There needs to be constant public pressure on our media to remind them that people are concerned about humanity and human issues. Just as politicians will often not deal with an issue unless it is a vote-catcher, so the media are concerned with what sells, and therefore it falls back into the hands of public opinion constantly to remind our society that we are concerned about moral issues and about justice and about those who are hungry.

Hungry for change

Oxfam launched a campaign called 'Hungry for Change' to try and encourage people to be consistently committed to bring pressure to bear on governments and society for long-term change. Their concern was to show that the problems of Ethiopia were better understood in the wider context of Third World poverty and of unjust global economic systems:

We have all seen horrifying pictures of Ethiopia today. But severe hunger is not confined to that one corner of Africa; five hundred million people go hungry ever day (that's the size of the entire population of Europe). Yet in the rich world many are reluctant to acknowledge responsibility; instead they prefer to blame world hunger on a convenient set of myths:

'There's not enough food' – wrong. The world produces enough food to give every person on earth a nourishing 3,000 calories a day.

'There are too many people' – wrong. Holland has 1,079 people per square mile, while Brazil, where thousands go hungry, has 39.

'We've got food mountains, why can't we send more food?' – we shouldn't. Food aid is essential for emergency relief, as in Ethiopia, but as a development tool it can upset local market prices and slow down the progression towards people feeding themselves. In reality, hunger is a condition which is fuelled by the influences and forces of rich countries like our own.

Two words, time-honoured members of the 'seven deadly sins', play a large part in the explanation of the current world food crisis, said Oxfam:

Avarice: In 1973 the price of oil doubled twice. Commercial banks, overwhelmed with surplus funds, channelled massive loans to the Third World and saddled them with floating interest rates. These interest rates have since soared so high that they have crippled many of the poorer nations. To cope with this crisis, these nations have been forced to make heavy cuts. And in human terms, the sacrifices have been severe. Health and social services, already basic, are now seriously threatened. Food prices have risen dramatically, wages have been reduced. And work is disappearing. These austerity measures have had a dire and often fatal effect on the poor.

Greed: The developed nations, comprising 30% of the world population, consume over 80% of its resources (not because they need to; the UK alone swallows over £500 million-worth of slimming aids every year). To satisfy this greed and at the same time pay the interest rates, developing nations have been forced to grow more crops for export. Consequently land that should be feeding their people is producing food for European and North American consumers. And thousands of acres are devoted to growing crops for European livestock, whose milk and butter end up as part of the rich world's food mountains. These systems lead to deprivation for millions. Scarcely able to feed themselves, the poor face a daily struggle to survive. Many don't. Every single day 40,000 children die as a result of hunger.
(from Oxfam, *Lessons to be Learned: Drought and Famine in Ethiopia*, Oxford 1984).

Graham Hancock, in his book *Ethiopia – The Challenge of Hunger* (Gollancz), after quoting extensively from that Oxfam report, then ends with these words:

Perhaps the Ethiopian famine has taught us that we can be apathetic no longer, that we cannot simply stand by and watch fellow human beings destroyed by avoidable hunger. Korem, Bati and Makalle – all have reminded us of a lasting truth: that we live in an inter-dependent world and that, in such a world, it is unacceptable for millions to starve, while others prosper.

The struggle still goes on. In Oxfam's fast of 7–9 November 1986, their main concern was to try and improve the terms of trade in favour of poor countries. Their particular slogan was, 'Did you know that for every £1 that we gave to Africa last year through government and voluntary donations, the West took back £2 in debt payment?' So while we ran, sang and appealed for money for African countries caught in the grip of famine, our governments, our financial institutions and our banks were extracting debt payments from those same countries. By the end of the year these amounted to £5,000 million – exactly twice as much as the money the world gave in relief aid!

Maybe we gave to 'Live Aid' out of charity – it's a good thing to feel compassion and to be charitable – but there's a further stage that needs to happen: we need to learn to cry out for justice. We can't keep emotionally responding to television pictures and tragedy, and what's more we should be building a world that tries to avoid these problems and starts to deal with the long-term issues.

The role of the church

It's in this area that the challenge for justice is paramount. Every church should be a voice against unjust trading systems. Justice has to be at the forefront of our Christian agenda if we're truly to echo the God of the Bible, who says, through the words of his prophet Isaiah:

> Is not this the kind of fasting I have chosen: to loose the chains of injustice and untie the cords of the yoke, to set the oppressed free and break every yoke? Is it not to share your food with the hungry and to provide the poor wanderer with shelter – when you see the naked, to clothe him . . . ? (Isaiah 58:6–7)

He goes on to point out that, 'If you do away with the yoke of oppression . . . and if you spend yourselves on behalf of the hungry and satisfy the needs of the oppressed, then your light will rise in the darkness, and your night will become like the noonday' (Isaiah 58:9–10).

Recent times have seen the rise of a strange doctrine – dubbed 'the prosperity doctrine' or 'the prosperity gospel' – in certain materialistic areas of western society, which suggests that if you follow God, he'll make you rich or bless you. In fact, the God of the Bible cries out for justice and an end to oppression. If we're involved in that, it has its own built-in blessing for the society and community – and for us – that starts to grow out of a world where people care for each other. But it is not a blessing measured in terms of personal material wealth or physical health. Often it will mean ranging ourselves against the status quo. It may well mean losing any wealth we may have had in the first place – but then we've been warned about storing up 'treasure on earth' (Matthew 6:19–21).

The Sudan experience made me feel anger, and I believe in the right sense it was a righteous anger. As I flew home on the plane and read that copy of the *Daily Telegraph*, there was another article by someone decrying 'Live Aid' simply because of musical snobbery – saying if he was starving to death he wouldn't want to be saved by money coming from music of this sort. I also read the passage I've already quoted about this country's record on giving and the way it had steadily gone down. Having just seen the sheer size of the problem, anger again bubbled up.

When I got home, I was told that Jonathan King had written an article in the *Sun* newspaper criticising 'Live Aid'. He said, 'I thought about the future for the people saved, and visualised civil wars, over-population, poverty, misery and millions more births.' He seemed to be suggesting that if 'Live Aid' was successful it would only make matters worse. Certainly that was how the article was interpreted when I was interviewed for the radio about my trip and they put the question to me, 'Why shouldn't people simply be allowed to die?' It is, of course, a most terrifying view. To suggest that people should be left to a fate like that is, of course, the Auschwitz syndrome again, one that fails to value human beings equally. For a start, it would be interesting to ask people their opinion as to whether *they* want to be allowed to live or die. Why should we continue to live, when we're enjoying a standard of living that is directly at the expense of the Third World and where we let others die simply so that our greed can be maintained?

We live in a century during which the value of human beings has been decried because of the suggestion that life is meaningless, that we're a collection of atoms that have no value. Such values can lead to this horrifying callousness. It's a hard line to maintain when you have actually talked to people in that situation and maybe even learnt their names (like Halima in Shagarab One). Then such victims stop just being 'millions' and they start to become people, and one realises one has no more right to survive than they do.

We need to recapture the vision of the poet John Donne (1572–1631): 'No man is an island, entire of itself; every man is a piece of the continent, a part of the main . . . any man's death diminishes me, because I am involved in mankind; and therefore never send to know for whom the bell tolls; it tolls for thee.' We are involved, we are interdependent. It is God's world and we're all part of his humanity.

I tried to express something of this same idea of John Donne's when I wrote 'No one is an Island', originally for BBC Radio Two's *Pause for Thought*:

No one is an island complete on his own
Each person's life must touch us too
So when you hear the bell toll, don't simply walk away
Remember that the bell rings out for you . . .

There's only one Father, who breathed His life in all
And planted His own likeness in each one
So when you turn your eyes away, turn and look again
Remember that you're looking at God's son.

To those whom much is given
So much will be required
A generous heart delights the heart of God
To those whom much is given
So much will be required
Loving hands reveal the mind of God.

BROKEN LAND

The rising sun from heaven
Came down on unbelief
To lead us out of darkness
Into the way of peace.

    Let peace and love come down
    Upon a broken land
    Let peace and love and justice flow
    And let's all take a stand.

Upon a barren hillside
Peace flowed down like rain
Broken hearts were mended
Healing out of pain.

    Let peace and love come down
    Upon a broken land
    Let peace and love and justice flow
    And let's all take a stand.

He walked among the lonely
And the poorest of the poor
Gave His life to save us
He lives for evermore

    Let peace and love come down
    Upon a broken land
    Let peace and love and justice flow
    And let's all take a stand.

8. BROKEN LAND – Northern Ireland

'Through violence you may murder the hater, but you do not murder the hate.'

Martin Luther King Jr

'If you believe what you like in the Gospel, and reject what you like, it is not the Gospel you believe, but yourself.'

St Augustine

'The violence we preach is not the violence of the sword, the violence of hatred. It is the violence of love, of brotherhood, the violence that wills to beat weapons into sickles for work.'

Archbishop Oscar Romero

'I believe that the one who can completely protect me is my Lord, Jesus Christ. If I want to carry a gun I have to reject Christianity.

This kind of thought, to many Christians in the Middle East, is simple nonsense, but we have been able to give an example in this area that we are real Christians and we live by the love of our Lord and by his teachings.'

Kamil Costandi, a Christian Palestinian Arab

A few years back, just before Christmas, I finished writing a song on the theme of peace. It was unusual because I hadn't written a Christmas song for about ten years, but I thought it was time for a fresh one. The chorus of the song went:

> Let peace come down this Christmas
> Upon a broken land
> Let peace come down this Christmastime
> And let's all take a stand.

I finished writing it, and set off for a concert I had that day in Liverpool. I took the words with me, even though I hadn't learnt the song. I didn't particularly intend singing it that night, but thought I might run it through during the sound check. As I went off, I said goodbye to my oldest boy, Tom, as he was going off to London with friends from a youth group at church. They were going to look at the Christmas decorations and at the shops, and they were starting off at Harrods.

A couple of hours later, as I was on the motorway, the news came through that a bomb had gone off at Harrods. I suppose it was the most shocking feeling I have ever experienced. I was about twenty miles from the nearest service station, and the feeling of helplessness and pain was simply overwhelming. By my calculations, Tom should have just arrived at Harrods. I prayed furiously that no one was hurt. The next bulletin that came in was to dismiss that thought.

When I arrived at the service station, I phoned home and was greeted with the news that he had already phoned in to say that he was all right. He arrived at Harrods literally a couple of minutes after the bomb blast. My enormous sense of gratitude was very quickly tempered by the thought of those very many other people equally shocked at the news who perhaps would not be as relieved as I was. Maybe they were, that night, greeted with the news of a death, maiming or injury of some sort. Indeed, shock itself is a kind of injury – a kind of stabbing inside – something seems to die.

I carried on and did the concert in Liverpool, and sang the song 'Broken Land' for the first time, sticking the words on the microphone stand and getting the audience to join with me in the chorus. We sang it as a prayer, thinking particularly of those bereaved or maimed as a result of the bomb, and I do not suppose I shall ever sing it in a more poignant situation. It is now a song that I've sung again and again in many varied places. It is no longer just a Christmas song. Its lyrics subtly change after the season of Christmas, to become:

Let peace and love come down
Upon a broken land
Let peace and love and justice flow
And let's all take a stand.

The 'Broken Land' tour

In September 1986 I did a tour of Ireland, both North and
South, called 'Broken Land'. This was at the invitation of
Youth for Christ, who asked me to do a tour picking up the
themes of reconciliation and peace, words which in a
curious way have come to be very devalued and even
disliked in the situation there. At that time, the Anglo-Irish
Agreement was proving deeply unpopular among the Protestant community, and therefore talk of peace was to many
people's ears a political statement – and one they did not
like. The poster for the tour had an outline of the map of
Ireland on it, and yet there was no divide across it. In
Ballymena, one graffiti artist chalked in the divide, at the
same time making a fairly abusive comment about 'a Brit'
on the poster.

'Peace' itself is sadly a much-abused word. The peace
people who demonstrate against nuclear weapons and
against wars often get abused, vilified and ridiculed, and
yet Jesus was described as 'The Prince of Peace', and said,
'Blessed are the peacemakers, for they will be called sons of
God' (Matthew 5:9). The word 'peace' or *shalom* means
'right relationships', and when we think about the word in
that context we immediately see how very deep it goes. On
a tour in Ireland one isn't just talking about the absence of
conflict, that itself does not bring peace. Peace always has to
be linked with justice – and that sometimes means actually
going back in time to try to analyse what are the causes of
wrong relationships within society, what are the causes of
injustice. To discover how the wounds occurred may not
solve the problem, but it may at least give us some idea of
how the problem came to be there, so in turn we can work
towards a just solution.

Trevor King, of Youth for Christ Northern Ireland, had

invited me to do these concerts and suggested the theme after a concert I had done a few months earlier in Lurgan. I was delighted to be asked to pick up the reconciliation theme, particularly by an organisation that is predominantly known as 'evangelistic'. Northern Ireland is probably the most over-evangelised part of the world – preacher after preacher comes offering personal salvation but apparently taking it no further. What it means to be a disciple of Jesus – to be a peacemaker – is rarely tackled.

What use are more sermons about Jesus? – it only takes his name in vain if people are not changed. If there is no repentance of the deep-seated prejudice and bigotry, then the gospel has not been received. If faith does not break down the old divides, then it is not faith. If the message preached does not challenge the divide, then it is not the gospel. As Jim Wallis points out, 'Evangelism that does not address the issues we face is not faithful evangelism.' Of course there are great reconciliation movements in Ireland, both North and South, such as Corrymeela or the Renewal Centre at Rostrevor, and many others, but their role is so significant exactly because they do take up the issue of what it means to be a follower of the Prince of Peace and not simply to mouth words about him.

The tour in Ireland was particularly a time of calling on people to repent, in fact calling on Christians to repent of not living out the Christian life. If one dares to use the name 'Christian', then it is not good enough simply to endorse cultural prejudice, rather we actually have to stand against the injustice that dominates that society.

Justice, peace and compassion go hand in hand. Many are scarred and brutalised by the continuing violence, and words like peace and reconciliation can seem like clichés or even slur words to some people. I called in the concerts for people to put Christ before Ulster or before the Republic – to surrender in a land where 'No Surrender' has become a source of pride. The way of the cross is a way of surrender; it is a rejection of arrogance and pride. It is the way of humility and turning the other cheek. It is riding on a donkey instead of a war horse. It is being vulnerable instead of powerful.

Despair and hope

I have visited Northern Ireland on many occasions, at least once a year for the last twelve years or so, and yet on this particular trip I felt very depressed during my first few days there. Nobody I talked to actually believed in the possibility of peace and it is depressing to be in an environment where nobody can see any way out. But for the Christian there is always hope, and that needs to motivate us in our role as peacemakers.

A few years ago, Bishop Desmond Tutu, as he was then, was interviewed on 'Heart of the Matter' by the BBC. It was, in a sense, a depressing interview. He was suggesting what the situation would be in South Africa in five years' time if people didn't bring pressure to bear on the government. In retrospect, it was a most profoundly prophetic interview, because exactly those things he was talking about have happened. The last question of the interview was, 'Well, don't you see any hope then?' and Bishop Tutu looked surprised, and said, 'Hope, oh yes, I see hope, because I believe in a man who was put to death on Good Friday, but on Easter Sunday he rose again.' This was how the programme ended.

There is hope, but it is not just a pious and vague hope with no action, as the life of someone like Archbishop Tutu shows. It is something that needs to be lived out in a practical way.

In Northern Ireland it calls for Christians to reject the injustice and immorality that is built into the sectarian divide – to walk across it and to embrace one another. There is a terrible price to pay for doing this as the vilification of the Presbyterian minister David Armstrong has shown in all-too-recent times. But I know of many others in that context who are equally bold, and brave, and committed to the love and justice of Jesus. They are determined that love will be seen in action and they are working for peace, for right relationships within the community.

It is a tragedy to see people who claim the name of Christ preaching bigotry and hatred, and listening to some of these people have been some of the saddest moments of my

111

life as I see the name of Christ dragged into the mud and him become a symbol of oppression rather than the symbol of freedom which the Bible reveals him to be.

The bitterness of bigotry

At one of the concerts, attended by a welcome mix of Protestants and Catholics, I was challenged by an irate Protestant at the end. Before I knew it, I was on the receiving end of a tirade of anti-Catholic abuse. He was particularly upset that I could suggest that Catholics could be followers of Jesus too, and that both sides should come together to meet, to talk and pray in small groups – one practical suggestion that I gave each night as a first step towards reconciliation. It is disturbing to meet the full force of bigotry – not I'm sure from a violent man, but from one who would claim to be deeply religious. After we had tried to discuss for fifteen minutes, he asked for half an hour more of my time to put me right, but I had had enough and said I must go. I left him yelling at me, 'Garth, you're wrong! Garth, you're wrong!' I was led away by a kindly man who apologised to me and then proceeded to tell me that in fact I *was* wrong, but that was because I was English and so could not be expected to understand.

Of course, there is some truth in that comment. The more I learn about Northern Ireland and its history, the less readily would I suggest a simple answer. In fact I have come to understand the quote Dervla Murphy put at the front of her book on Northern Ireland, *A Place Apart* – 'I have yet to see any problem, however complicated, which when you looked at it the right way did not become still more complicated' (Paul Anderson). It is in a sense a humorous, slightly cynical and fatalistic comment, yet at the end of the book – a book which, incidentally, paints a very affectionate picture of the North – she says: 'Only one sure prediction can be made about the present Irish Troubles: they will not go away tomorrow, or the day after. No political initiatives or amended legislation or constitutional juggling can bring true peace to Northern Ireland until its people have changed within themselves.'

The cross says 'change'

It is exactly at this point where the message of the cross is so relevant, because it calls on people to change – to sacrifice, to repent, to turn away from their deepest prejudices – and also provides the motivation and resources to do so.

In an interview with John Coulter in *The Newsletter*, a Northern Ireland Protestant newspaper, while I was on the tour, I commented:

> You have got to take the initiative away from the person who shouts the loudest, espouses hatred and violence and the gunmen.
>
> The people who take this initiative are very often the humble, ordinary people who will come out and kneel and pray or sing in the street together – and say, we will not allow this to continue in our society.
>
> This is a movement that can succeed in Northern Ireland, but it needs the backing of the churches.
>
> Either Christianity is going to be slurred forever by the religious divide, or else there is going to be a great turnaround by the churches if they link together and their people come out at great cost to themselves.

Peter Cotterell, a London Bible College lecturer, recently took up this theme. In an open letter to the Protestants of Northern Ireland, published in the Christian magazine *Today* (December 1986), after fifteen years of preaching in Ulster, he writes:

> I must tell you that because of you the name of 'Protestant' is spoken against all over the world. I have had your activities hurled at me by Marxists in Ethiopia, by atheists in Australia, by Catholics in America. If what you have been doing in Ulster is Protestant Christianity, then the rest of us will have to find a new name for ourselves . . .
>
> What is needed in Ulster is a Christian Bob Geldof to say in simple, blunt language that the violence must stop. That it doesn't have the support of the Church. No matter

what, Protestants of Ulster, are you for violence? For if you are then know that we are against you, because the Book for which you profess so much regard is against you. If you live by the sword you will perish by the sword. And rightly so.

'No surrender!' I've heard it again and again. And from across the water we've watched it all on our TV screens once again, and we tell you: enough!

Christians are to forgive. To forgive as God, for Christ's sake, has forgiven us. But your marches won't allow you to forgive. They are the Protestant Ulsterman's unholy communion, that ensures that old enmities, old bitternesses are not forgotten, old wounds are not healed . . .

The Peace People

Back in 1976, the Peace People, or Peace Women, had rallies in Northern Ireland and in the UK. On 27 November they came to Trafalgar Square. I sang at the rally, in fact it was my role to sing as the march was coming into the Square. The opposition from the Troops Out Movement was already in the Square, so I was basically left entertaining them while waiting for the first of the marchers. I started to sing a song called 'Walk in His Shoes'. I didn't explain the song, and it doesn't refer by name to Jesus, but I based it on words that Mother Teresa had written as a meditation about the passage in Matthew 25 and then linked it in with words that Jesus had quoted from the prophet Isaiah:

Walk in His Shoes

When I was hungry you gave me to eat
When I was thirsty you gave me to drink
When I was homeless you opened up your door
When I was naked you gave me your coat
When I was weary you helped me find rest
When I was anxious you calmed all my fears
When I was little you taught me how to read
When I was lonely you gave me your love.

He's a friend of the poor, he brings good news
A friend of the oppressed, he walks in their shoes
He marches for justice and for those born to lose
He's the healer of the broken, confused and abused
And those of us who follow him must walk in his shoes.

When in a prison you came to my cell
When on a sickbed you cared for my needs
In a strange country you made me feel at home
Seeking employment you found me a job
Hurt in a battle you bound up my wounds
Searching for kindness you held out your hand
When I was aged you bothered to smile
When I was restless you listened and you cared.

He's a friend of the poor, he brings good news
A friend of the oppressed, he walks in their shoes
He marches for justice and for those born to lose
He's the healer of the broken, confused and abused
And those of us who follow him must walk in his shoes.

You saw me covered with dirt and with blood
Yet you knew my features though grimy with sweat
When I was laughed at you were standing by my side
When I was happy you shared in my joy.

He's a friend of the poor, he brings good news
A friend of the oppressed, he walks in their shoes
He marches for justice and for those born to lose
He's the healer of the broken, confused and abused
And those of us who follow him must walk in his shoes.

© Word (UK) Ltd.

As I was singing the song, I became aware that there was a chant building up among the opposition. Gradually it dawned on me what they were saying: they were chanting, 'We want Barabbas – we want Barabbas.' It was the most profound and intellectual piece of heckling that I have ever come across – not only did they recognise who the song was about, but they were letting me know that they stood for the opposition.

I will always recall that rally as the time when I first began to understand the deep hatred that those seeking peace can arouse in their opponents. The hatred was never clearer than when Lady Jane Ewart-Biggs, the wife of the British Ambassador to Dublin who had only recently been shot, got up to address the crowds. The undisguised shouts of, 'We'll get you just like we got your husband' were sickening to hear. The truth dawned on me that we were in a spiritual battle against the forces of bitterness and evil.

Joan Baez also sang at the rally, and she too came in for harsh criticism, yet she is someone who has always been utterly consistent on her pacifist stance and her commitment to peace.

As I was going away from the rally, I was grabbed by one of the opposition demonstrators, who said, 'Were you just singing in the rally?' I said 'Yes,' and he said, 'What, peace at any cost?' I replied, 'No, not peace at any cost. I believe in peace with justice.' He looked surprised and left me at that.

We live in a very wounded world, but it's a world that needs to listen. We need to learn to listen to one another. Shouting slogans is very easy, and it is often hard to be a peacemaker who actually dialogues with the other side. Northern Ireland desperately needs that style of Christian who will give up their own prejudices, walk across the barriers and divide, and become part of Christ's healing mission in that society.

Peace like a phoenix

I wrote a song after the Peace People's rally in Trafalgar Square in 1976 that became one of the theme songs of the reconciliation tour ten years later:

> From the ashes of yesterday's dreams, we long to see you rise
> Wipe the tears from your eyes
> Oh the bitterness that salts your wounds, let it wash away
> Let's hear you say, let's hear you say.
>
> Let peace like a phoenix rise again
> Let tears of forgiveness fall like rain
> Let there be a new breath in the valley of death
> Let peace like a phoenix rise again.
>
> With your hand wipe away the hatred that we see
> Father of all, set us free
> With the sword that sheds no blood, break the pride and let there bud
> A tree of life, a tree of life.

Let peace like a phoenix rise again
Let tears of forgiveness fall like rain
Let there be a new breath in the valley of death
Let peace like a phoenix rise again.

On the rubble and the pain, send a healing rain
Let your love, let it smile again
Nobody seems to listen although they use your name
Lord your death seems all in vain.

Let peace like a phoenix rise again
Let tears of forgiveness fall like rain
Let there be a new breath in the valley of death
Let peace like a phoenix rise again.

A day in Belfast

On the 1986 tour we spent a morning driving round some of
the notorious areas of Belfast – it is like entering another
country altogether. The ashes and pain of the bitterness
and hatred have left indelible scars. It is like exploring the
set of a war movie, so closely at times does it resemble one's
imaginary picture of a war-zone in the 1980s. The windows
of shops are boarded up or covered with fencing, the small
packs of nervous British soldiers patrol key areas, the
critical shopping areas are out of bounds at certain times of
day and prowled by heavy security at all times in an effort to
lower the chances of more bombs. This description only fits
certain areas, of course, and it is possible to live in Northern
Ireland – and in Belfast itself – and be almost unaffected by
'the Troubles'. Similarly the people hustling and bustling to
the shops do not look as if they live in a war situation. They
have grown used to this way of life, they have grown used
to their constant enemy – 'the Troubles'.

But the reason it most resembles a film like, for instance,
Under Fire, which is set in Nicaragua, is that in key Catholic
areas, massive, eerily beautiful murals have been thrown
on to the walls of the bleak streets: reminiscent of the style
of revolution that many Northern Ireland Protestants fear
for their own country. There are scenes of the ordinary
peasant or worker, turned soldier or rebel against an

oppressive regime, with a romantic-looking rifle slung over his – or her – shoulder. The oppressor, naturally enough in this case, is cast as the British government and its forces of law and order in the form of the British Army. You know when you have turned into a Protestant area, as the style of mural changes dramatically. The hand of Ulster, the Bible and the Union Jack come well to the fore.

Our tour took us past the notorious Divis flats, a strongly Republican area where hundreds of young children, as Trevor King explained, have never met a Protestant. They can't. They're too scared. The broken-down, dilapidated housing; the ugly graffiti and stray, scraggy, uncared-for animals; the pathetic figures of children making the best of a bad job by playing in the gutters – all of them betrayed the reality of their country's war situation.

Those troubles are not merely the guns and bombs and armoured cars, the ugly threats and sectarian murders and shopping-centre bomb-blasts, they are not merely the 'ends justifies the means' philosophy that sees innocent people knee-capped or policemen gunned down. No – behind the horrific headlines and beneath the veneer of war is a small country which in some respects, unrecorded by the media, is a Third World country inside the United Kingdom.

We drove down the infamous Falls Road, where the Catholic population on one side had purposely erected massive steel fencing in order not merely to protect them-selves from stones or missiles from the Protestant area across the road, but so that they should not even have to look, not even have to see, the Protestant 'land'. The interior of Belfast seems to have exploded with church buildings at one time, many of which are now dilapidated, empty or boarded up. It still remains true that the area has the highest proportion of mission halls and buildings for public worship per head of population in the entire world.

The children bear the scars

The faces of the children tell a story. Trevor told us that in one recent riot the average age of the participants was eight years old. They could have little, if any, idea of the real reason for the fighting, and were only expressing the hatred bred into them by their sectarian parents – Catholic or Protestant – since birth. One little girl of nine, Trevor recounted, the daughter of a Royal Ulster Constabulary policeman, was recently taken for a day out in the country by her cousin. Near the end of an enjoyable day away from the city, she went into a local newsagents to buy some sweets. As she glanced at the evening newspaper on the counter, she saw to her horror that it carried a photo of the bloodied, dead face of her father, victim of an IRA bomb. The banner headline read, 'RUC Man Blown to Death'.

'Those sort of scars never heal,' Trevor lamented, 'she'll always hate the Catholics.'

The 'Broken Land' tour was sometimes a difficult one, with an element of tension close to the surface, but it always seemed eminently worthwhile and the warmth of response was heartening and sometimes deeply moving. Three days of concerts down in Eire, in Dublin, Cork and Galway in the South, was a relaxed and joyful break that seemed a world away from the feuding of the North – then we headed back north to Omagh for the final concert, back into the society where the hard slogan, 'Ulster says No' was casting its shadow.

No gospel to proclaim

Much of the content and thinking that lay at the heart of my presentation in the 'Broken Land' tour was sparked off by a previous visit to Northern Ireland. On that occasion I had been involved in some reconciliation meetings organised by the Presbyterians with two speakers, one, John Perkins, a black speaker from the USA who runs an organisation over there called Voice of Calvary Ministries, which works in some of the most depressing inner-city and ghetto areas. The other speaker was Chris Sugden, who runs the Oxford Centre for Mission Studies.

John Perkins had a dramatic and fascinating story to tell. As a black man born in Mississippi, he had experienced the results of racial oppression and segregation. His brother had been killed in a racial incident. He himself had been beaten up brutally in a police cell, and so the story goes on.

Though he left Mississippi and went to California, on becoming a Christian he felt it was right to return and try to share the gospel. He returned to Mississippi and found the prejudice the same as when he left it. Saddest of all, he found the churches the strongest proponents of prejudice. He discovered the truth of Martin Luther King's statement that, 'Eleven o'clock on Sunday morning is America's most divided hour.'

Having decided that black and white must work together, he started approaching white ministers to try and get them to cooperate. After talking to one such minister about working out the message of the gospel together, the white minister agreed that he would do this with him, but he said, 'Give me three months so I can preach to my congregation from the Bible and explain to them the message of the gospel and the theme of reconciliation.' After three months that minister committed suicide as his congregation had so decisively rejected that message.

He started again with another minister. It came round to lunchtime. The minister felt he could not take him home because of what his people would think. He could not take him to a restaurant because the restaurants were segregated, so John and his wife were given five dollars to go and get lunch. When they met up again with the minister after lunch, John said to him, 'We have no gospel to proclaim.' The message of the gospel was negated by their segregation. The division between them was a denial of the result of the gospel, that 'in Christ there is neither Jew nor Greek, slave nor free'. They had no message to proclaim to a needy world because they had not taken that message to heart themselves.

As John told this story every night in Northern Ireland, those words hit me forcibly each time: 'No gospel to proclaim.' The gospel is about reconciliation. Reconciliation between God and man, and between man and man. If we segregate racially, economically or over religion, we deny the gospel. There is actually no message, because our lives deny our words.

Obviously John's story carried great poignancy and challenge in the religiously-segregated situation in Ireland. It also carries enormous force on every level – our world is economically segregated between rich and poor, so is our country. The church seems to flourish best among the well off. Why is this, when Jesus came to bring good news to the poor?

It is because we have not really shown how the values of the kingdom actually stop people being poor. In other words, the church has not redistributed its wealth and challenged society to do the same. It has become a church of the status quo. We have offered personal peace to the poor to help take their minds off their poverty, but we have not offered justice and a new way of life in reality, so the gospel has not had any force with them: they have not seen the gospel, they have not seen Jesus.

John Perkins says in his book *With Justice for All*:

> The only purpose of the Gospel is to reconcile people to God and to each other. A Gospel that doesn't reconcile is not a Christian Gospel at all. But . . . it seems as if we don't really believe that. We don't really believe that the proof of our discipleship is that we love one another (John 13:35). No, we think that the proof is in numbers, church attendance, decision cards. Even if our 'converts' continue to hate each other, even if they will not worship with their brothers and sisters in Christ, we point to their 'conversion' as evidence of the Gospel's success. We have substituted a gospel of church growth for a gospel of reconciliation.

Sadly, many times churches have actually been against the gospel because of their endorsement of divides, as in the Northern Ireland situation between Catholic and Protestant, and in the South African situation where white churches have often accepted, and sometimes even tried to justify, the apartheid system. So God is being used to prop up worldly views of division. We have made him in our own image and it is horrible to behold. It is tragically a world full of scars, but the cross is the event that is at the heart of the healing, at the heart of the possibility of peace.

LIGHT A CANDLE IN THE DARKNESS

It was raining down in Memphis
On the night before he died
A shot of hate would come tomorrow
Maybe that's why the heavens cried.

   Light a candle in the darkness
   Light a candle in the night
   Let the love of Jesus light us
   Light a candle in the night.

On a Wednesday in Kampala
There they shot Janani down
He stood firm against the evil
He paid the price he won the crown.

It was on a Monday evening
In the town San Salvador
That he took the fatal bullet
All because he loved the poor.

   Light a candle in the darkness
   Light a candle in the night
   Let the love of Jesus light us
   Light a candle in the night.

The world grew dark upon a Friday
Creation held its breath in fear
By the wounds that He was given
We are healed if we draw near.

Angels sang upon a Sunday
The devil moaned and turned aside
A blaze of glory from an empty tomb
Death itself has had to die.

   Light a candle in the darkness
   Light a candle in the night
   Let the love of Jesus light us
   Light a candle in the night.

9. LIGHT A CANDLE IN THE DARKNESS

>   Not in the palaces
>   of the Princes
>   and the Priests
>   who live
>   by tradition
>   and kill
>   the innocents
>
>   But in the homes
>   and hiding-places
>   of the poor
>   and persecuted
>
>   We find the King
>   Who was born to be
>   their Brother.
>
>   And worship him.
>
>   Sue Elkins

'I believe that only the Church can stop the arms race now. Without the consent and support of the Christian community the arms race could not continue. Our greatest political hope is for the churches of East and West to regain the biblical vision of the body of Christ, which knows no boundaries of race, nation, or ideology but lives in the world as a community of reconciliation. The people of God could unite to create the moral force to stop the insanity of the world's political wisdom, leading the way to peace. Christians could refuse to cooperate with our nation's nuclear policies, obstruct war-making plans, and point to alternatives for real security.

But the way to peace will be the way of the cross for those who choose to be peacemakers. It was for Jesus, and it will be for all those who follow his path.'

Jim Wallis

Martin Luther King once said, 'We shall have to repent in this generation not so much for the evil deeds of the wicked people, but for the appalling silence of the good people.' As I had sat in that Chadian refugee camp at Senna in the Sudan, I had felt anger that as Christians we had done so little to assert the worth of human beings by our deeds. By our words we assert incredible value for each person, because we claim each one is made in God's image, but our lives have not been showing it, and I had this great fear of the silence of the Christian church on many of the big issues where our world is hurting.

Because I had to come back and prepare a Christmas presentation, even as I sat in that camp at Senna, I couldn't help thinking about the message of the incarnation (i.e. when God became man) and the fact that he didn't come in wealth and power and grandeur, that he rejected status, that he came as a helpless baby, born into poverty, soon a refugee. Somehow his identification with those who are at the hurting end of the world suddenly took on a new meaning as I sat in that camp. I wrote a second set of words for the 'Candle in the Darkness' song that particularly put an emphasis on the Christmas message:

> Like a flicker in the darkness
> Comes a mother's desperate cry
> Then a baby's voice in answer
> Brings the coming of the light.
>
> > Light a candle in the darkness
> > Light a candle in the night
> > Let the love of Jesus light us
> > Light a candle in the night.
>
> He did not come in wealth and grandeur
> He did not stand with men of power
> He had no status to commend Him
> He was homeless – He was poor.
>
> But He came to heal the wounded
> And He came to heal the scars
> Of a world that's bruised and broken
> Where the image has been marred.

124

And we see Him in the hungry
And the homeless refugee
In the sick and dying children
His hands reach out to you and me.

And I feel His breath upon me
And He whispers 'follow me'
And He grants His fire within me
Says 'let it shine for all to see'.

So light a candle in the darkness
Light a candle in the night
Let the love of Jesus light us
Light a candle in the night.

The Bible is a painfully challenging book. It doesn't just call for people who assent to things in their head, it calls for disciples of Jesus. The message of Christmas is one so easily lost and so easily relegated to one part of the year, and yet it gives us a profound insight into God's heart and mind. The birth of a baby means new life in more than the literal sense. Its arrival brings joy and new possibilities.

The birth of Jesus, of course, is a supreme sign of hope and celebration for our broken and wounded world. 'His kingdom will always be at peace,' writes Isaiah. 'He will rule as King David's successor, basing his power on right and justice' (Isaiah 9:7 GNB). Our God not only sees, cares and stands with those who suffer, but he has brought in a kingdom committed to the rule of justice, peace and hope. As Christians we are called to be part of this community – fighting against the oppression, exploitation and greed which surround us. Our celebrations of Christmas should somehow reflect God's bias to the poor.

Jesus in the poor

Shortly before I left for the Sudan, I took part in a young people's leadership conference. One of the speakers was American sociologist Tony Campolo, who constantly reminded us that 'Jesus is incarnated – made flesh – in the poor.' I couldn't help thinking of those words when I was with the Ethiopian refugees and the Chadian refugees in

125

the Sudan. There was an echo of Jesus' own statement that, 'whenever you [do] this for one of the least important of these brothers of mine, you [do] it for me' (Matthew 25:40 GNB). There is an irony here. When Jesus talks about 'the least important' he speaks in a 'worldly' way, similar to the terms we use to refer to those we think of as our inferiors. But he then goes on to invest an enormous amount of value in these people by saying we can find him in them and serve him by serving them. It is a message we need constantly to remind ourselves of, especially, and perhaps surprisingly, when we're helping others or giving aid. It is so easy to patronise people and thereby devalue them. Seeing Christ in each one helps us to give them the respect they deserve.

Martyrs of our time

It was a book by Mary Craig called *Candles in the Dark*, thereby echoing the theme of being lights in a dark world, that first prompted the writing of my first version of 'Light a Candle in the Darkness'. The book was written about six modern martyrs whose lives were certainly lights, and it was dwelling on three of the individuals in this book that first prompted me to write the song. In February 1977, Janani Luwum, Archbishop of Uganda, was murdered during Idi Amin's terrible regime in that country, and the Dean and Chapter of Canterbury Cathedral decided to set aside a chapel in memory of martyrs of our times. During the visit of Pope John Paul to Canterbury Cathedral in May 1982 there was a very moving ceremony where various leaders, including the Archbishop of Canterbury and the Pope, took candles and lit one in memory of a particular martyr. Each of them spoke aloud the name of one martyr and then placed the lighted candle in a seven-branched candlestick.

Mary Craig then wrote the book that took up the story of these different martyrs. In my song I include three of them. First of all, I put a focus on Martin Luther King, because of the influence he had been on me by his example. Then I move on to Archbishop Janani Luwum, and then finally to Archbishop Oscar Romero of San Salvador.

Oscar Romero

Oscar Romero was shot on 24 March 1984 as he preached in his own cathedral in San Salvador. A fascinating man, he became a champion of the poor in a country where poverty and injustice are a way of life. Yet he was put into office because it was thought that he would not 'rock the boat'. It was not to be the case. His commitment to the gospel was too strong, and it became the dominant theme of his ministry. Archbishop Dom Helder Camara of Brazil has said, 'When I give food to the poor they call me a saint, when I ask why the poor have no food they call me a communist.' If we are going to be light in the darkness, we have actually to question the darkness, to question the oppression that keeps people in poverty and in pain.

Oscar Romero is an inspiration. To read his sermons is fascinating, as he grapples with the issues and as the two-edged sword of the gospel meets those issues. He says:

> What marks the genuine Church is when the Word, burning like the word of the prophets, proclaims to the people and denounces; proclaims God's wonders to be believed and venerated, and denounces the sins of those who oppose God's reign, so that they may tear those sins out of their hearts, out of their societies, out of their laws – out of the structures that oppress, that imprison, that violate the rights of God and humanity. This is the hard service of the Word.

Non-violence

Romero is an important man to learn from, not only because of the passion of his commitment, but also because of his desire to use the right methods to achieve his ends. In other words, he saw the important truth that 'the means are the end':

> As Christians formed in the Gospel, you have the right to organise, to make concrete decisions inspired by the Gospel. But be very careful not to betray those evangelical, Christian, supernatural convictions in the company

of those who seek other liberations that can be merely economic, temporal, political. Even though working for liberation along with those who hold other ideologies, Christians must cling to their original liberation (19 June 1977).

He was totally against all forms of violence, whether it was the aggressive terrorism of the security forces and the state, or the violence of the revolution, but he went to the root cause and he saw that it was the institutionalised violence of the country in which he lived.

Poverty and violence are injustice and aggression. An unjust silence is again a temptation at this point. Most people throw up their hands in horror at one so-called terrorist act, while keeping completely quiet about the institutionalised violence that happens day by day in many countries. When we hear of an explosion in South Africa, we need to ask 'Why?' – and the answer is so obvious. When we hear of a horrendous massacre by Palestinian terrorists, though we must deplore it, the question has to be asked of Israel, America and all of us, 'But what is the world going to do about the Palestinians who have no nation?' Oscar Romero talked about this, and said, 'The violence we preach is not the violence of the sword, the violence of hatred. It is the violence of love, of brotherhood, the violence that wills to beat weapons into sickles for work' (27 November 1977). The overwhelming power of non-violence has only rarely been tried, by such people as Gandhi or Martin Luther King Jr.

What is the gospel?

Sometimes when I've been on one of my journeys in the Third World and have been in situations of poverty and suffering, I've asked myself the question, 'What is the gospel?' As I look at the Christian church, I see Christians narrow it down to something personal and pietistic. I ask the question particularly because there are some of us who would be happy to be called 'gospel singers' if that word were actually defined, but we can only claim that title if we actually apply the relevance of Christ's gospel to the world in which we live. Oscar Romero says:

> We cannot segregate God's Word from the historical reality in which it is proclaimed. That would not be God's Word. The Bible would just be a pious history book in our library. It is God's Word because it enlightens, contrasts, repudiates, praises, what is going on today in this society (27 November 1977).

As the prophet Isaiah says:

> When you spread out your hands in prayer, I will hide my eyes from you; even if you offer many prayers, I will not listen. Your hands are full of blood; wash and make yourself clean. Take your evil deeds out of my sight! Stop doing wrong, learn to do right! Seek justice, encourage the oppressed. Defend the cause of the fatherless, plead the case of the widow (Isaiah 1:15–17).

And then he goes into that famous passage, '"Come now, let us reason together," says the Lord. "Though your sins are like scarlet, they shall be as white as snow . . ."' (Isaiah 1:18). So often we've interpreted that verse as if it is applied to our individual sins, whereas it comes into the context of a discussion where God condemns the whole of Israel's worship because they allow injustice to survive.

They're still hungry in Africa. The blasphemous regime still exists in South Africa. The Palestinians still have no homeland. Millions are spent creating nuclear weapons while two-thirds of the world go to bed hungry each night. Four million refugees have been forced to flee from Afghanistan as a result of what the Russians are doing there. The other superpower has created an army to try and destabilise the Nicaraguan government. No one's hands are clean. And in our own land we see increasing division as certain areas of our country get poorer, while others don't feel the pinch. Unemployment is far higher among black and Asian young people than among white young people. This is the challenge before the silent community. These are the days to speak up. These are the days to light candles in the darkness.

129

A hat raised for dignity

Perhaps by quoting people who've become martyrs as examples of those who have allowed their light to shine, it can give us the impression that they are a special brand of people, perhaps even saints, and we find it hard to relate that to ordinary life. Of course, the truth is they are ordinary people with feet of clay like any one of us, and one of the strengths of Mary Craig's book *Candles in the Dark* is that you see their feet of clay.

It's not just the great causes that challenge us to be lights in our world, it's the day-by-day way we treat one another, it's the act of personal dignity.

Some years back in South Africa, a young black lad waited in a hospital with his mother. In came a white priest who raised his hat to the young lad's mother. This lad, Desmond, had never ever seen any white man treat his mother with respect before. It was to be a turning point in his life. Later that priest visited him every week when he was in hospital for 20 months. It was instrumental in bringing him to faith. He is now the Archbishop of Cape Town, Archbishop Desmond Tutu. The simple act of Trevor Huddleston of showing respect to another human being was an act of letting the light of Christ shine for a moment into that situation. It was an act which was to have a quite amazing result, in bringing to faith a person whose Christian witness has in turn been an example all around the world.

The life of prayer

To be examples, to be those who reflect the life of Christ in any given situation, in ordinary, everyday life, demands lives of prayer and worship. Too often in our churches our worship and our prayer times are very parochial and very introverted. Perhaps we even need to rediscover some ritual and symbolism to help us with our prayers. Maybe we need to start lighting candles for wounded and hurting parts of our world, and for parts of our society.

There is a very moving passage at the end of a chapter in Tom Davies' book, *Stained Glass Hours*, in which he says:

The steady and bright flame of a candle tells us much about that which is holy. It tells us about the unbroken flow of prayer which continues even after our private prayers have stopped. It tells of the light that Christ brings into our lives and into the lives of people we meet . . . I took a candle and lit one . . . for embattled Ulster, in the prayer that a great ball of purifying fires would be rolled across the province, and that its frightened children be delivered up from the coils of this evil snake, as, even now, it continues trying to squeeze the last vestiges of life from the community.

With the weeping rage of God in me, I lit another that his province might one day be delivered from the shadow of this man of lawlessness; that God might send all his holy angels to put an end to the weeping and dry all the tears . . . I lit another with Elijah in mind, who, after years of prayer and hope, saw the first clouds of rain on the horizon, after a long, long drought.

God is racked with pain at this attack on his babies so we should all be lighting candles throughout Ulster that the hate now ebbs away, and that this thing should come to an end. Jesus said, 'I am the light of the world.'

As Tom puts across in his passionate and poetic style something of his own concern to bring healing in the broken society of Northern Ireland, perhaps he has captured something that as churches we need to be doing. We need to be acting out a helpful ritual that will cause us to pray, and as we do this, and as we capture a sight of the wounded areas, as we pray for them in turn, it will challenge us to action.

When people ask me what we should do in the face of huge problems in our world, I believe we need to form prayer-and-action groups within our churches, because one person at a time cannot cope with all these issues, we can't even hold the issues in our mind. Some of us have good memories, others simply can't hold certain facts, and yet within every church there are different gifts, and we can encourage one another and challenge one another as to how we should act, how we can reflect Christ's heart and mind, how we can be lights in our immediate society and wider afield.

131

We live in a time when it is easy to see how interrelated our world is, it reminds us that it's God's world, and that each decision made has implications both near at home and far away. Worship has got to start reflecting God's incarnation once again; in other words, it must start to relate to his world. Every one of us has a part to play in this; it's the little act that can often mean so much.

The European drought

Through my journeys in the Third World I've learnt so much. As I've looked at people's material povery, I've often seen their wealth in areas of spiritual life and community life, and it's given me a changed view of my own society.

One certainly sees a drought in terms of spiritual life as one looks across Europe, with its bankrupt philosophies of this century suggesting that God is dead and that therefore human beings have no significance and worth. This attitude not only affects the way we treat other people, it affects the way we build our cities, it affects the way we treat the environment.

We have a desperate need within Europe for a spiritual refreshment and rediscovery, and the joy and the friendship and the community life of those parts of the world that we so often call 'Third World' have made me very aware of this.

Perhaps that very term, Third World, is a tricky one. There are some who would now prefer to use the term 'Two-Thirds World', in other words reflecting the reality of the quantity of the world that we're talking about, rather than the first, second, third aspect as if we were somehow in some kind of a race – a race which economically the first world may be winning, but which certainly it isn't winning in terms of community or spiritual life.

Living the gospel

One aspect that I've learnt about the gospel from the Third World – or Two-Thirds World – is not to divide between evangelism, or proclamation of the gospel, and social action. The two are to be seen as totally integrated and we need to learn from them to bring these two back into harness again.

To share the gospel is not just doing something with your mouth, it is actually something to be lived. I think of Bishop Misaeri Kauma, and his wife Geraldine in Uganda, and their commitment to the widows, orphans and to the refugees, and yet their desire to share the gospel with words as well. Whenever I am with them I think of James 1:27, where it says, 'Religion that God our Father accepts as pure and faultless is this: to look after orphans and widows in their distress and to keep oneself from being polluted by the world.' This integrated gospel needs to become a part of our lifestyle.

Meeting with Christians in that situation has made me take seriously the Bible, and hopefully to grow up as an individual. I remember once talking with Cliff Richard about our experiences travelling in Third World situations (for many years he has done trips for Tear Fund – he's been to Bangladesh, Africa and, more recently, to Haiti). I asked him what he felt was the impact of these trips, and especially his first trip, and his reply confirmed very much the way I felt. He said, 'I just felt I grew up.' This was what happened to me in 1982 when I went to Uganda and saw the daily conflict and struggle that so many people live under, and then later that year stood in Calcutta and saw the thousands upon thousands struggling to survive in the streets there; I realised I had to take more seriously the realities of this world: I had to grow up and become committed. This is not a world where it's possible to stand on the sidelines, you're on one side or the other.

Perhaps it is not quite accurate to put the date of my growing-up to 1982. I remember after going to Haiti in 1978 being deeply challenged to take the Bible more seriously. When I came back I read an article by Richard Adams, now the Director of Traidcraft, who was talking about the way we try to duck the hard issues of the Bible. In fact the article made me realise how often we spiritualise away some of the truths of the Bible and fail to take them literally. We distort

133

the words of Jesus particularly when they're uncomfortable. As a result of the Haiti trip and that article I wrote the song, 'How Hard':

> How hard for the rich man to enter the Kingdom
> How hard it is to survive
> How hard were the words that Jesus spoke to him
> 'Give it up if you want to have life.'
>
> How hard for the rich man to enter the Kingdom
> Like a camel through a needle's eye
> How easy to keep it and go away sad
> A high price to pay just to die.
>
>> How easy to change what he said
>> To shuffle the words till they're dead
>> How easy to pull out the sting
>> Leave a saccharin saviour who's wearing a grin.
>
> How hard for the rich world to share what it stole
> And give it away to the poor.
> How hard for me, how hard for you
> To obey the words of the Lord.
>
> How poor is the rich man who says he's been blessed
> By the Lord for the wealth that he hoards
> How poor is the rich man who's doing his best
> To justify serving two lords.
>
>> How easy to change what he said
>> To shuffle the words till they're dead
>> How easy to pull out the sting
>> Leave a saccharin saviour who's wearing a grin.
>
> How hard for the rich man to enter the Kingdom
> And have wealth that means so much more
> How hard for me, how hard for you
> To obey the words of the Lord.

The simple lifestyle

When I was in Kenya and saw the simple lifestyle of the Pokot there, it made me think about our own lifestyle. They were suffering the results of drought and so they were in a particularly desperate situation, but the actual style of life, had it not been for the immediate crisis, was one which was somehow happier and more satisfactory than our own. I did a lot of thinking as to why this was. They are not bombarded with adverts, they are not surrounded by shops – there is just one store and they barter with each other – and they seem somehow more satisfied because of the lack of the greed pressure. Community life was very strong; sexual morality was very strong. Something clicked for me in that situation, and I thought, a simpler life is actually a better life.

Now we can't all go and live like the Pokot, and it would be wrong to romanticise their society, because, of course, every society has its problems and its tensions, but there is a lesson to learn that we need to incorporate. One of the problems of our society is overindulgence, and that occurs at every level, whether it is eating, drinking, clothing, or toys for children at Christmas. We've only got to analyse what we tend to call 'needs' to realise just how few real needs there are. We need to view our churches more as communities – i.e. not communes, but where we learn to live in walking distance of our churches and in closer proximity to one another, so we can start to share possessions and hang loose to a lot of things that now we feel are essential. This will all help us to get spiritually fit.

The problem of riches

I remember doing a new year's eve television programme with Malcolm Muggeridge several years back now, and I found him absolutely fascinating. He's a man with a great enjoyment of life, and with a sparkle in his eye like a hobbit, but he realised the actual benefit of abstinence. It is good for us sometimes to fast; it is good for us to strip ourselves down to the minimum, you actually enjoy life more fully.

This brings us back to the situation of the rich young ruler. Contemporary Christian wisdom would often say to the rich man, 'Keep what you have, don't change your lifestyle, but become a Christian. You can be a good influence among the rich.' We go to a powerful man in society and say, 'Great, we need a powerful man, stay exactly where you are and join some special Christians winning other rich and powerful people for the Lord.' Nobody is asked to change except in the area of personal sins. If the rich man has a mistress, we tell him to stop it (which is absolutely correct), but when Jesus loves a rich man he offers him the best that he can possibly give him, by saying, 'Go, sell your possessions and give to the poor . . . Then come, follow me' (Matthew 19:21). He stresses how hard it is for a rich man to enter the kingdom of heaven. The disciples are stunned, and say, 'Who then can be saved?' (Matthew 19:25). We are frightened to say you really do have a problem with riches because they can strangle and throttle your spiritual life. We want the rich and the powerful on our side, but that isn't the way God works. He says of the church: 'Not many of you were wise by human standards; not many were influential; not many were of noble birth. But God chose the foolish things of the world to shame the wise; God chose the weak things of the world to shame the strong. He chose the lowly things of this world and the despised things and the things that are not – to nullify the things that are . . .' (1 Cor 1:26) The method God uses is completely opposite.

Showbiz Christianity

This also relates in the areas of music and show-business Christianity. We think if we get 'stars' of one sort or another – great sports people or great singers or actors or whatever – on to a platform, people will say, 'They've become Christians, so we'll become Christians.' We are wanting to commend the faith in terms of worldly stars, whereas what we should be saying to people is, 'Come to an alternative, because Jesus offers you something that is much richer.'

Putting up a rich and successful person can actually create the impression, 'I can keep all of that, but I can also have a bonus as well, which is Jesus.' That is not what we should be saying. We should be saying, 'Come to someone who is the pearl of great price: he so dominates everything else that you'll sell everything else and give up everything else in order to have him. He will completely and radically change your life.'

Now I'm not saying that everyone has to give away all their possessions and their wealth, because it isn't that simple, and one of the hardest things is to be stewards of possessions and wealth, but I do think we have to get away from the worldly view that rich and powerful people will help us to influence for Christ. They're the very ones who might need to hear the helpful words, 'Give it up, and reject the power that wealth brings. Put your trust in the power of Christ.'

The sermon on the mount is the key to so much of this. 'Blessed are the peacemakers. . .' said Jesus, yet we tend to think, 'Blessed are the powerful', which is why we put our confidence in bombs rather than in the cross of Jesus. The church is a community of *shalom* – or right relationships – that should be an agent of restoring those relationships within wider society. We can't do that if we put our faith in worldly methods of power and status. It is not the Christian way.

> He did not come in wealth and grandeur
> He did not stand with men of power
> He had no status to commend Him
> He was homeless – He was poor.

Christians occasionally do speak up. It was amazing how the Christian community rallied over the Sunday trading issue and became a very powerful voice, writing to their members of Parliament. People were standing up in churches advocating that we should do so. It seems harder to motivate Christians to sustain the pressure on the hunger issue, and even harder still when people can duck behind that word 'political', as if somehow God is not interested if you can put the political label over a particular issue. So the churches have kept a low profile over the issue of nuclear weapons, over the issue of the environment, over the issue of South Africa.

The war against the poor

I remember sitting on a train, travelling with commuters back from London, on the day that the main news story on the front page of the evening newspaper was about the Cruise missiles being based in this country. As I saw the headlines, the tears came involuntarily to my eyes, I thought, 'What have we done? – we have not spoken up, we have not stopped these terrible weapons of destruction, we've let them come trundling in and yet it's the nuclear weapons that are killing people, not by being used but simply by being created.' As Jim Wallis has put it, 'The bombs are already falling in the war against the poor.'

I remember singing one night in Amarillo, Texas, and I was particularly putting a focus on the hunger issue. When I came off stage and was talking to people afterwards, I realised the terrible irony of the situation: down the road they were making five or six nuclear bombs every single day, each one of which made the bomb dropped at Hiroshima look tiny in comparison. And somewhere in the USSR there's an Amarillo where the same story is being repeated. It's the very use of resources in this direction that means that less is spent on the poor and needy. The mere fact that we're making bombs, and spending millions doing so in a world where two-thirds go to bed hungry, is an indication of how far we've fallen away from what's right and what's just.

The making of the nuclear bombs is the supreme folly. After all, we can't possibly use them all, we would have destroyed the world long ago with even the use of a few of them, and yet the greatest brains are used to create these weapons of evil, whereas they could be turned to do something to bring healing over the hunger issue or over issues of disease. In our own country we've seen the defence spending go higher and higher, while the spending on welfare issues has become more and more obviously needed. The divides in our society are exaggerated by the Defence Budget soaring so high. Our taxes are being used to build up the stockpiles of weapons, when in fact even a cursory glance at our inner-city areas shows how badly the resources are needed there. Injustice of this nature breeds problems for the future.

Poverty at home

In the autumn of 1984, I was on tour for Scripture Union, doing a presentation called *The Bride*. We were playing in many towns and situations where tours don't normally go – it was a deliberate policy. This was the winter of the miners' strike, and we played several mining areas. It was heartbreaking to see the division, the conflict and the suffering that this dispute was causing. But did we really ever get to hear the truth of that dispute?

I remember in Wales, in one area, talking with people about the pit that their whole community had been built around, and they told me they wouldn't give in over the strike because they knew their pit was on the hit list, so they had nothing to lose by the strike. When I arrived there, shops were closing because of the lack of trade. One man told me how his wife used to work in a store there, so they survived OK for the first part of the strike, but now she had been laid off because the shop had closed. Later I heard that the pit had indeed closed after the people had gone back to work. The community was destroyed.

Economics has been ruling our thinking and as E. F. Schumacher pointed out, we need to do 'economics as if people matter'. If economics determine that a certain industry around which a community is based must go, then it is not enough simply to close it, we have to find an alternative for that community before we have the moral right to close it. This will take time, it may be economically frustrating, but there is a moral obligation not to destroy people and their society.

Peacemaking in our own society sometimes gets more opposition than peacemaking further afield. In other words, people don't mind money being raised for the hungry, but they don't like to bring pressure beyond that charitable giving of aid. I remember after touring in the autumn of 1984 talking to a Christian organisation about making an audio-visual to put a spotlight on the poverty in our own country. They received it with enthusiasm, but in the end it was turned down by one of their general committee, who said that he wouldn't want his youth group to watch it. Strangely enough, he lived in a town which was soon to erupt in a riot of violence because of the tensions building within our inner-city areas.

There's none around here

Some years back, I was involved in making a filmstrip called *There's None Around Here* which dealt with the question of racism and was particularly geared to those areas where there are not many ethnic minorities. Consequently people are able to say, 'There's none around here,' and assume that they have no racial problems, whereas in those areas there is normally an absolute groundswell of racism which is reflected in voting patterns and attitudes.

We live in a society where racism is mounting within our inner-city areas, but the attitudes of racism are to be found in our tabloid newspapers and they are to be found right at the heart of our middle-class areas. I am staggered both by the virtually colonialist jokes that are still cracked and by the constant inability to see black and Asian people as British.

Recently there was a Church of England Report on Racism, and I happened to pick up a copy of the *Daily Mail* on the day it came out. The editorial was one of total abuse of those who had produced the Report, on the grounds that it was another example of the church being trendy and dabbling in things that it had no right to dabble in. In fact it pointed out that if the church had done its duty (i.e. spiritually speaking), the problems in our society would not exist. It was a most extraordinary divide between sacred and secular, as if somehow God isn't interested in racial issues, but if you convert people to some sort of spirituality suddenly all these problems will be solved. Of course, the two-edged sword of the gospel is pointing out the injustice of racism that riddles our society, and that is painful and it makes us yell, but unless it's done the disease will still be right at the root of society.

The church cannot be a light if it is ignoring the issues. Recently a woman came up to me and told me how she'd been ridiculed by members of her own church because she is a member of Christian CND and had demonstrated down at Molesworth. She was thanking me for my songs and the fact that they'd encouraged her to keep on doing her work for peace. But it saddened me that she was getting laughed at right at the heart of her church simply because she was being a disciple of the Prince of Peace. What she was doing may look foolish to many, but then we were always told that we should be fools for Christ's sake, and as we take up the cause of being peacemakers and as we reflect the light of Jesus, there will be many who find it foolish.

> He died to say we're valued
> He died to show our worth
> He died to say 'I love you'
> To every soul on earth
> And every unjust system
> Each evil deed that's sown
> Each person who's devalued
> Is another nail knocked home.

('Litany for Africa')

The cross says how much we're valued and how much we're worth. It reminds us how we should treat other people. The cross cuts away the prejudice at the heart of our lives, it brings the possibility of forgiveness, it is the compulsion that reminds us we must forgive. It brings us to our knees in repentance over our wrong attitudes, but it also picks us up and shows us the route we must follow, the style of life we must pursue. It challenges us to be those who live for peace; those who bring healing because we've been healed of our own bitterness; those who pray; those who act; those who refuse to keep silent, because we have glimpsed the way of hope and the way of Jesus; those who let that light shine, who light that candle even though it may seem a faltering light – even though it may seem an insignificant contribution, it is nevertheless a desperately needed light in a very dark world.

141

WATER OFF A DUCK'S BACK

Here come the Prophet quickly run away
We don't want to hear what the Prophet say
Cover up your ears, close your eyes real tight
In case he starts talking about the wrong and right.

   Like water off a duck's back everytime he spoke
   Treat him like a maniac, treat him like a joke
   Like water off a duck's back everytime he spoke
   Treat him like a maniac, treat him like a joke.

I see the gleam of your military machine
It's treasure on earth it's a frightening scene
Your poor go hungry but can you even see
For where your treasure is there your heart will be.

   Like water off a duck's back . . .

Your guns don't impress me, your speeches much less
Most folk are dead, but they don't know it yet
While the Bishops and the Priests play Russian Roulette
There's only one way to get out of debt.

   Like water off a duck's back . . .

Lightning like an epitaph right across the sky
Do I hear the thunder as it rumbles in the night?
Did I see an angel check his watch as he went by?
Right across the universe I think I hear a sigh.

Blessed are the pure in heart for they shall see God

Blessed are the peacemakers for they shall be called the sons
   of God

Blessed are the meek for they shall inherit the earth

Blessed are the merciful for they shall obtain mercy

10. WATER OFF A DUCK'S BACK

'Only a God who suffers can save us.'

Dietrich Bonhoeffer

'We need to be the kind of Church which tries to obey the word of God for both rich and poor . . . The Church is one of the few bridges which can reach across to different sides of our polarised community. It is part of our reconciling task to help different groups to listen to what the others perceive to be happening.'

Bishop David Sheppard

'We do not want, as the newspapers say, a Church that will move with the world. We want a Church that will move the world.'

G. K. Chesterton

It was Eastertime 1984, the start of Holy Week, and I stood looking up at one of the most bizarre monuments to religion that must exist in our modern world, the Crystal Cathedral in Los Angeles.

The Crystal Cathedral is the brainchild of TV evangelist Robert Schuller, who specialises in a doctrine called possibility thinking. His positive line of psychological encouragement beams its way to millions every Sunday and proves very popular as he redefines sin as 'lack of self-esteem'. Possibility thinking has led him to spend $15 million building a great big, glass church . . . right on the San Andreas Fault!

The Crystal Cathedral is a striking and also ridiculous piece of architecture. Glass is a very cold material with little or no character. After observing that it is a clever design and that it is more or less a spectacle like many skyscrapers that grace the skyline of most US cities, what else is there to say about this greenhouse of psychological religion? Here there is no sense of awe and majesty, no sense of the loving care and dedication that is so evident in many older cathedrals. That is not to say that it was not built with loving care, it's just that glass does not carry the imprints. It shows no expression. It looks like a quick twentieth-century instant cathedral – a quick gasp, and then on to Disneyland, significantly close by.

Does Disneyland give us the clue as to how to interpret Schullerland? There is a track on T-Bone Burnett's album, *Proof through the Night*, called 'Hefner and Disney', in which he speculates on two characters who encourage people to live in fantasy worlds and thereby take away people's genuine ability to dream. He locates them in a world called 'Never-Wonderland' and describes them as 'dupes of the wicked king who wanted to rob the children of their dreams'. It is a brilliant track, as he deliberately confuses the activities of these two fantasy-world makers, thereby revealing the pornography of excess that symbolises the self-indulgence at the heart of a materialistic world.

Schullerland is a sort of Christian Disneyland. The night I was there they were presenting an Easter special called 'The Glory of Easter'. It was extraordinary – a kind of full-scale passion play. Horses, sheep, goats and even a camel were lining up for the spectacle. I watched as a Roman centurion mounted his horse at the second attempt, looking incongruous with a cigarette dangling from his bottom lip. For $10 or $12 tickets you could go inside and see this spectacle of Easter. I could not resist the desire to investigate. Not having a ticket proved a problem, but the English accent and a look of wonder on my face marked me out as a tourist to be impressed. Fingers all pointed me to the ticket office, but when I explained my schedule did not allow this, I was granted a peek into the very heart of Schullerland itself. They waited expectantly for my response: 'Wow!' I exclaimed ambiguously.

It is actually a curious place with a ceiling design that looks as if the scaffolding might still be up. A purple carpet marked out a raised platform for tonight's performance. One of the ushers promised me they would hold a ticket for me for the next night. 'Thank you,' I smiled. It seemed no barrier to them that, as I had already explained, I would be in Phoenix, Arizona. There's possibility thinking for you!

By now it was dusk outside, and odd characters looking as if they had stepped out of Sunday school pictures were turning up. Any resemblance to reality seemed far away. The world of 'Never-Wonderland' was about to spell it out for another night, and dispel a few truths and mysteries. A sanitised, packaged, easily-digestible Christianity for the bourgeoisie to feel blessed.

'If Jesus first described his ministry as "good news to the poor", what is the message of this place?' I asked my companion. I won't quote his reply. He had just returned from a visit to Haiti and the memory of thousands in real poverty was too painful and too close. 'It's obscene,' he concluded, eyeing this monument to materialistic TV religion. I started walking away, wondering how God's real creative hand could break through in this imitation version. At that moment the tail of one of the centurions' horses went up, and a horse fiercely and noisily defecated. I was doubled up with delight; reality does break through in any fantasy world. My spirits were considerably lifted, though I did feel a twinge of regret: if only the horse had waited for the purple carpet . . .

The lights were now on in the Crystal Cathedral and the show had started. As my friend and I stood looking at the presentation as it appeared through one of the glass walls, an enthusiastic teenager came up to us: 'If you think these lights are good, wait till you see the boom-booms.' 'The boom-booms?' enquired my friend. 'Yes, the incredible boom-boom lights when Jesus dies.' I turned away, sickened. It seemed the ultimate blasphemy – the death of Jesus subordinated to a lighting effect. Is this where commercialised Christianity has brought us? Easter in Schullerland was not Easter for me. Show business it may be, but this is not the Easter faith to heal a broken world.

Easter came for me in Baton Rouge, Louisiana. I was on tour, doing support to Phil Keaggy, an American guitarist and gospel artist. We were going right across the southern states of America, and then heading up north. My particular set was to put a spotlight on the work of Compassion, an American relief and development agency. After our concert at Baton Rouge, Phil took me to the house of Geoff Pollard, a friend who had been a professional musician. He played us two or three songs, and then he played us a version of 'When I Survey the Wondrous Cross'. It was a tune I was not familiar with, and I have never heard it sung with such conviction. He was in tears as he sang it, there was nothing false or contrived here, but genuine tears and pain and wonder.

> When I survey the wondrous Cross,
> On which the Prince of glory died,
> My richest gain I count but loss,
> And pour contempt on all my pride.
>
> Forbid it, Lord, that I should boast
> Save in the cross of Christ my God;
> All the vain things that charm me most,
> I sacrifice them to his Blood.

We were a world away from 'Never-Wonderland', and we caught a glimpse again of truth and mystery. In the humility of the singer, and in his rejection of his previously self-indulgent and materialistic way of life, I saw something of what it means to be a disciple.

So Much Better

> What have we done to you
> I bow my head in shame
> We've sold you so far short
> Misused your precious name
> Took away the holiness
> Took away the fear
> Watered down your words of truth
> Try to twist your arm in prayer.
>
> To obey is so much better
> To obey is so much better
> To obey is so much better
> Every time.

146

I see those TV preachers
Holy 'get-you-rich-quick' teachers
Like pre-digested TV dinners
Offer instant salvation packs for sinners
Put your hand on the TV screen
Makes God look like a slot-machine
Is this really what you meant
By your costly blood-bought covenant?

What do you require from me
Is it something new?
Then he led me back in time
To words forever true
The worship I desire from you
Is that you do what is right
Show mercy and show love
And walk humbly in God's sight.

The cross of Christ

The cross of Christ gives the key to our response to the pain
and suffering of our world, and the words quoted earlier in
the book from Micah 6:8 are vital words for the modern
church. They come in a discussion on worship, and it's as if
the people are asking God what sort of worship he requires,
and the answer is almost, 'I've told you so many times': 'He
has showed you, O man, what is good. And what does the
Lord require of you? To act justly and to love mercy and to
walk humbly with your God.'

Unless we obey, and unless we take up the lifestyle of the
cross, I can't see that we'll even begin to be credible as
Christians in the contemporary world. Sometimes I'm
asked how these journeys that I've done in the Third World
have affected me personally, how can I actually cope after
what I've seen? I've talked with some people who say they
can't believe in God any longer in the light of what they've
seen, because there's so much suffering in the world.
Strangely enough, it's pushed me the other way, because
even in the middle of suffering I've caught a glimpse of
God, and it's only him and his strength that gives meaning

and also gives hope in situations of such desperate despair. Harry Blamires, in his book *Where do we stand?*, has an interesting comment on the problem of suffering. He says:

> If there is no God, there is nothing remarkable about suffering, and therefore its existence does not pose a problem. It is irrational to say, 'I can't believe in God because of suffering,' because without God the existence of suffering is not a problem but only a fact. It becomes a problem – something that needs to be specifically explained and accounted for – only when you have accepted that there is a good God at the back of everything. Indeed, if one may so put it, the better the God, the more difficult it seems at first sight to explain why His world should contain so much misery. That is why Christians must always feel especially sympathetic towards those people who say to us, 'I can't believe in God, not after what has happened to me or mine – not since my brother was killed in an accident, not since my daughter died of paralysis.' People who argue thus are already half believers in God, or they would not have need to make this protest. Without a basic, instinctive sense of a purposed Universe, they would have no cause for indignation. They would accept suffering as the kind of thing to be expected in a world produced by chance. Their protest springs from a deep sense that there should be, ought to be, love and sympathy and conscious purpose at the back of everything, and not blind chance which is indifferent to pain.

I think it is, in fact, the faith that I've seen under suffering that has helped me at least to cope with it better, and not simply howl with despair. I think of Grace, in the township of Graaf-Reniet, whose husband had become permanently handicapped by being tortured by the Security Forces, who was working to relieve the suffering in a situation of tremendous poverty and whose life shone with the love of Jesus and gave hope to all she met. This was a triumph in the face of suffering, and her love of God and her perseverance refreshed my faith.

The God who suffers

It may not be fully understandable, but we have a God who seems to identify with those who suffer and who are oppressed. The style of his birth shows us his rejection of wealth and status and power, and we see his identification with the poor and the refugee. The style of his death reminds us that he stands with those who suffer. His name, Emmanuel, means 'God with us', and God is with his world in its suffering. At the same time, he reminded us that as we see people who are hungry and sick and naked, who are prisoners, who are thirsty, who are strangers, it is as we minister to them that we reach out to God. This is our way of showing love to God. It is at this point that the challenge to the church becomes amazingly powerful. John Stott, in his book *The Cross of Christ*, says,

> I could never myself believe in God, if it were not for the cross. The only God I believe in is the One Nietzsche ridiculed as 'God on the cross'. In the real world of pain, how could one worship a God who was immune to it? I have entered many Buddhist temples in different Asian countries and stood respectfully before the statue of the Buddha, his legs crossed, arms folded, eyes closed, the ghost of a smile playing round his mouth, a remote look on his face, detached from the agonies of the world. But each time after a while I have had to turn away. And in imagination I have turned instead to that lonely, twisted, tortured figure on the cross, nails through hands and feet, back lacerated, limbs wrenched, brow bleeding from thorn-pricks, mouth dry and intolerably thirsty, plunged in God-forsaken darkness. That is the God for me! He laid aside his immunity to pain. He entered our world of flesh and blood, tears and death. He suffered for us. Our sufferings become more manageable in the light of his. There is still a question mark against human suffering, but over it we boldly stamp another mark, the cross which symbolizes divine suffering.

Bishop Festo Kivengere

'God with us' is the great mystery and the great hope at the centre of our faith. Bishop Festo Kivengere was telling me of a time he visited a refugee camp on the border of Uganda and Rwanda. In fact it was not technically a refugee camp because the people weren't classified as refugees: both countries rejected them, and they didn't even have the status of refugee. It was Bishop Kivengere who helped to bring it to the notice of the United Nations. He told me that as he walked around the camp he was utterly shocked and appalled by the conditions and quite distraught, but many of the people in the camp were Christians, and they held a little service and began to sing, and the song they were singing said, 'where God is there is joy', and they clapped their hands, and they said, 'where God is there is laughter', and they laughed. Festo said he just couldn't believe it and he went to one woman afterwards and said, 'How can you possibly praise God in this situation?' and she smiled, and said to Him, 'You see, Bishop, you come and visit us, and then you go away again, but Jesus never leaves the camp.'

Joy in suffering

I have seen that when everything else is stripped away, when all the props that we take for granted so easily in our lives disappear, what is left is the reality of God. We may not understand the suffering, but we see what really matters in life and what is of deep meaning.

In Uganda in 1982 I found that my faith was suddenly revitalised through the lives of those who showed such a deep love to God in a most traumatic situation, and who not only spoke of him with love but acted in love to their brothers and sisters who were suffering. One word could sum up that visit, 'joy': not a superficial happiness, but a deep joy always born out of suffering; a deep joy born out of a resurrection faith.

In my experience, those who are dealing most with those who suffer seem to have that sparkle of joy. Watching the face of someone like Archbishop Tutu, as he proclaims that he's a man of hope because he believes in Someone who was put to death on Good Friday, but who rose again on Easter Sunday, makes me see that same commitment to justice and to compassion and to joy that seems to identify such people. When I was with Mother Teresa and saw the sparkling eyes and the humour in her face I realised the same thing. She told me, 'We won't take on people who are prone to depression.' She said, 'There's enough sadness already in the situation here, we want people whose lives are marked by joy.' Similarly when I think of Bishop Misaeri Kauma and his wife Geraldine, whose home has been such a haven and inspiration to so many people, their deep and profound love of God is always marked by the sparkle of humour and joy. Those who have known God in suffering seem also to know the joy and refreshment that he brings. Perhaps because they see with the eyes of eternity and have also glimpsed something of the heart of this deeply compassionate God who went to the cross.

Jesus of the scars

It is this extraordinary wounded God who speaks to our wounded world. To me it's a mystery and yet I know it to be true. John Stott quotes a poem by Edward Shillito. It was a poem published just after the First World War. Overwhelmed by the carnage, nevertheless the poet found inspiration in the scars of Jesus Christ, and the poem is called 'Jesus of the Scars':

> If we have never sought, we seek thee now;
> Thine eyes burn through the dark, our only stars;
> We must have sight of thorn-marks on thy brow,
> We must have thee, O Jesus of the scars.

> The heavens frighten us; they are too calm;
> In all the universe we have no place.
> Our wounds are hurting us; where is the balm?
> Lord Jesus, by thy scars we know thy grace.

> If, when the doors are shut, thou drawest near,
> Only reveal those hands, that side of thine;
> We know today what wounds are, have no fear;
> Show us thy scars, we know the countersign.

The other gods were strong; but thou wast weak;
They rode, but thou didst stumble to a throne;
But to our wounds only God's wounds can speak,
And not a god has wounds, but thou alone.

Rediscovering humanity

In suffering there is an insight into the character of God. It
may not solve all our intellectual reasoning, but we find he
is there and it gives us an example to follow.

We live in a century when God has been devalued. At the
end of the last century Nietzsche could say 'God is dead'
and suggest that we've outlived the need for God. Many
others have taken up that cry during this century, but if
God is dead, so are humans, because what is the value and
worth of a human being unless he is created and made in
the image of God? Unfortunately, too many people have
suggested we're simply here by chance, we're just animals;
and that's the way we've come to treat people. We need to
rediscover faith; in turn we will then rediscover the worth
of a human being. There is a drought in our society – a
drought of spirituality, which in turn affects community
life. There are two reasons: we've lost sight of the worth and
value of each person, because in turn we've lost sight of the
creator. In rediscovering God we shall rediscover humanity.

The church as the body of Christ

Although my faith in God has been strengthened, I have
sometimes felt anger at the church. I shall never forget
sitting in the refugee camp in Senna, where a quarter of the
children had died in the previous month, and thinking,
why is the church so silent and so self-indulgent? I have met
many, many good Christian workers who have been busily
working away to alleviate suffering for many years, but the
church as a whole has not cried out as it should have done
against the injustice of the poverty of the Third World. It
took the extraordinary outburst of Bob Geldof to challenge
the world. As one reads his book *Is That It?*, one can't help
but see the hand of God using this rough but compassion-

ate character to challenge a complacent world. Though Bob doesn't profess belief in God, at one point he himself almost looks bemused at the way things began to come together. Maybe God was tiring of the politeness of his church and its inactivity.

The church is called to be the body of Christ, to be the family of God, to reflect the heart and mind of Jesus. We're called to be bricks that, built together, form a building where God can dwell and feel at ease, so that when people come into that community they see something of the character of God, and are able to say, 'Ah, that's what he's like.' But we've lost sight of the building of this community, consequently people can't see God's character. God is at work in his world, and it's time for his church to catch up with him.

The church seems to be caught in the trap of old-fashioned ritualistic worship, or the trap of modern 'charismatic' worship with its endless and mindless choruses that endorse pietism and little more. We need our history and our heritage, and we need our warmth and life, but our style of worship determines the way we live, and I believe God is still saying, 'I hate, I despise your religious activities, because you endorse injustice and you keep the poor poor by the system of life that you are a part of.'

We are part of a world that spends millions on nuclear bombs and uses the cleverest brains to make them, while two-thirds of the world go hungry. We're part of a world that takes back from the Third World more than it ever gives in voluntary contributions, because of the debts and the way the trade tariffs are set up. It is simply not good enough. It's time for the church to say 'No! We will not compromise.'

God proved to us that he is interested in the real issues. He came down to earth. Our worship must come down to earth. As we take the Communion, if we ignore our brothers and sisters who are dying of starvation and injustice, then we are eating and drinking judgment to ourselves because the Communion, of all places, should be the point at which we remember those of the body of Christ who are suffering.

153

Worship in the real world

Recently I had a letter from a black pastor in South Africa who has a church in Soweto. He said this:

The recent shooting of some thirty people just one and a half blocks away from our home, because they refused to pay rent as a protest against the State of Emergency, involved me in some really dangerous situations. It started when the Police tried to evict some of the people in the middle of the night, and hundreds of young people gathered to help those people. Then the Police started shooting at point blank range. I had made several house visits, and was taking two young men home at about 9.00 p.m., when I found myself surrounded by over five hundred young people who were stoning cars, but mine was not stoned, and I was able to chat with them. The shooting went on for six hours, and apart from those killed, over ninety people were injured. Because I live in the area, I was part of the committee of priests and ministers who arranged the planned mass funeral. One day, before this was to take place, it was banned by the authorities. Early on the day we went to the stadium where two to three thousand mourners had gathered, to tell them to go home. But the Army was already there. We pleaded with the officers to allow us to dismiss the people (instead of the Police chasing them with tear gas and sjamboks [leather whips]). But one soldier, right in front of us ministers, panicked and threatened to shoot us – I thought my last moment on earth had come. The Police secretly buried fourteen of the dead people (after confiscating all the bodies earlier), without the families knowing anything. The next day we decided to bury the remaining twelve, but were allowed to take only one coffin into the cemetery at a time, with twenty mourners. Thus it took us from 8.00 a.m. to 2.00 p.m. until all were buried. Although forbidden by the Police to do so, we sang a hymn and prayer at the burial of the last coffin, and suddenly found ourselves surrounded by soldiers with their guns loaded and pointing at us! But God protected us again, and we were able to drive home safely, though utterly exhausted. Yet this is nothing compared to the trauma the bereaved families experienced, having not only lost their – often quite young – children, but having every custom and tradition related to the burial of family members disrupted by the Police.

That is the reality of pastoring in a suffering world.

If our worship reflects only selfish interests, then it does not have the attitude of Christ. At the heart of our worship must be compassion for his world; our worship is not just something to be done in church, it must be lived out. We have to be those who take up the issues of justice and peace in a tangible way.

We need a new reformation within the church, a biblical movement. In a recent interview in New Zealand I was trying to point out my own motivation in what I'm trying to challenge Christians to do, and I said, 'I'm trying to challenge the Christian community to a consistency of life. I have a vision of a great, vibrant, loving, laughing, lively creative community that challenges the world, laughs at its folly, speaks out at its injustices, and brings healing and hope.'

We have to reject the temptation to silence. Our voice has to be heard in society, speaking with prophetic power. In our worship we need songs that sing about real life, prayers that pray about real life, real exposition of the Bible that relates to real life. Our worship has betrayed us, our evangelism has been utterly incomplete. We must introduce people to God and to his character, so that they in turn become followers of the way of the cross.

Recently I've been forcibly reminded of wounds in our own society, not least in the journey around Northern Ireland, but also up in Edinburgh while doing a concert to launch a centre for the unemployed in a town that has the highest crime rate in Europe, mainly because of the drug situation, which in turn has led to the highest incidence of AIDS outside London. The centre that was doing such valuable work there was struggling from month to month, not knowing whether or not the workers could be paid.

This is exactly the sort of work the church should be doing in a deeply wounded urban situation like that.

Just recently I did a concert in a church right next to Brixton. It was a fabulous evening from my point of view, because it reminded me of the sort of community the church should be. It was entirely multiracial, with people from very varied backgrounds, but I was particularly struck by the way in which they involved handicapped people in the life of the church, and the way everyone was able to accept them so easily. Just to walk into that community gave you some idea of the healing and reconciling role of the gospel.

What can I do?

I am conscious that merely to look at some of the great needs of our world freezes some people in inactivity; they think, How can we solve this problem? Perhaps they are stunned by the sheer size of the problem. In reality we simply need to start doing something. I think of one person who, through listening to my song 'Oscar Romero', decided she ought to set up Amnesty International in their area, and just recently I went back to do a concert in aid of Amnesty.

I've heard from others who have organised Tear Fund lunches and started to inform people about the reality of the suffering of the Third World. Some have got involved in selling Traidcraft or Tearcraft products, others have started campaigning as part of the peace movement, for Christian CND or Evangelical Peacemakers. Still others have started to do something about the unemployed in their neighbourhood, and I've heard of one white doctor and his wife who have gone to live and work in a black township in South Africa.

We cannot change the world on our own, but we can do something, and we are part of a community that, because it is called to be the body of Christ, can change the world. As Terry Waite says, 'I refuse to believe that we cannot make this world a better place. I do, though, firmly believe that we can only make a difference through the small efforts of man, millions of people – starting with you and me.'

For action

As we plan our worship, we need to realise that our agenda should be God's agenda, and we should look at his world and see where the suffering is at its deepest, because we know that God will be involved exactly at that point. We need to identify the areas of need in our own communities, so that we know what, within our own context, the good news to the poor is.

For practical action, maybe each one of us needs to come to the Communion or Eucharist in repentance. It may be helpful to make a list of our prejudices – because all of us have certain prejudices that we have been brought up with and we need to identify them. They can be prejudices of racism, sexism, greed, or simply the prejudice of not opening our eyes to the needs of God's world. We need to repent. We need to make sure that we're converted in every area of life.

Then we need to form prayer and action groups within our churches to motivate them to show the love of God to the real world. It's time to stop our worship from betraying us, from simply endorsing our prejudices and helping us to preserve the status quo. It's time to realise that following Jesus is a passionate commitment or nothing at all. It's time to take up our cross and to get on the road of discipleship and it is going to need changes at the deepest level. We need churches that burn with passion for the hurt parts of our society and world; they will in turn become churches of deep joy as Christ refreshes us. Our liturgies need to reflect our commitment.

The Lima Liturgy

Here then, in closing, are a few words from the prayer of intercession in the *Feast of Life*, which is the Lima Liturgy produced by the World Council of Churches:

In faith, let us pray to God our Father, His Son Jesus Christ,
and the Holy Spirit.

For the Church of God throughout all the world, let us invoke
the Spirit and the diversity of gifts.

Lord, have mercy;
Christ, have mercy;
Lord, have mercy;

For the leaders of nations, that they may establish and defend
justice and peace, let us pray for the wisdom of God.

Lord, have mercy . . .

For those who suffer oppression or violence, let us invoke the
power of the Deliverer.

Lord, have mercy . . .

Across the barriers that divide race from race, reconcile us,
O Christ, by your cross.

Lord, have mercy . . .

Across the barriers that divide the rich from the poor,
reconcile us, O Christ, by your cross.

Lord, have mercy . . .

Across the barriers that divide Christians, reconcile us,
O Christ, by your cross.

Lord, have mercy . . .

Across the barriers that divide men and women, young and
old, reconcile us, O Christ, by your cross.

Lord, have mercy . . .

Confront us, O Christ, with the hidden prejudices and fears
which deny and betray our prayers. Enable us to see the
causes of strife; remove from us all false sense of
superiority. Teach us to grow in unity with all God's
children.

Into your hands, O Lord, we commend all for whom we pray,
trusting in your mercy, now and forever. Amen.

POSTSCRIPT (OCTOBER 1986) – back to Uganda

It was exhilarating to be back in Uganda to be receiving that same heartwarming welcome we experienced previously.

We were in a village called Namisambia, in the Diocese of Busoga, where there is a church called Bishop Hannington. We were there on 29 October, which is the anniversary of his death, for a special service. When we arrived we were welcomed with singing and dancing performed by the local Mothers' Union. It was an incredible atmosphere.

In the service, David Prior, the leader of our team, spoke and I sang 'A Candle in the Darkness' which with its reference to Archbishop Janani Luwum, had a particular poignancy in that setting. Since the service was to celebrate the death of the first Christian martyr in Uganda, it was perhaps fitting that a much more recent martyr should also be remembered. At the end of the service I sang my song 'Namirembe', and the whole congregation joined in, singing and dancing, and in the end I led them outside. It was an exuberant moment. Then in the gathering gloom we had to take up the challenge of a football match against the local team – we were soundly thrashed, to the delight of the local village. Then it was off to be fed a special meal.

Since I was only out there for a short visit, to sing in schools and colleges as part of the Busoga Diocese's celebrations of the centenary of Bishop Hannington's death, I didn't think I'd have a chance to get into Kampala, and back to Namirembe, where Bishop Misaeri and Geraldine Kauma live. But Ugandan Airlines had other plans for me, and the plane was delayed for twenty-four hours, so I was able to go and spend a night at Misaeri and Geraldine's home. There I had the privilege that I'd always valued so much on the previous visit, of being part of their evening prayers. Misaeri shared some of the experiences at the time of the recent coup when the previous government's army was retreating. It was a desperate time, and several times they had to flee from their house and try to hide in the nearby bush as the soldiers came searching. They had up to eighty-five refugees staying in their home at one time. He said how everyone had clung to Psalm 121. As a word of encouragement to other Christians, they would simply call out: 'Psalm 121.'

I lift up my eyes to the hills –
   where does my help come from?
My help comes from the Lord,
   the Maker of heaven and earth.

He will not let your foot slip –
   he who watches over you will not slumber;
indeed, he who watches over Israel
   will neither slumber nor sleep.

The Lord watches over you –
   the Lord is your shade at your right hand;
the sun will not harm you by day,
   nor the moon by night.

The Lord will keep you from all harm –
   he will watch over your life;
the Lord will watch over your coming and going
   both now and for evermore.

Misaeri and Geraldine seemed tired; they had obviously been through the most devastating of years – yet one more in a pattern of very devastating years – but still their home was such a centre of faith and warmth. Prayer ended that night, as it always does in Misaeri's household, with the singing of a little song that he has written. The lyrics go, 'What is impossible to man is possible with God. Amen.'

In a world that cries out for meaning, in a world that cries out for hope, in a world that cries out for justice, for peace, there is a way of reconciliation, there is a way of healing. It is the joyful road of obedience, the joyful road of being a servant of Christ: the painful and prophetic road of being a member of his community.

The church has been asleep, perhaps in the chains of materialism, perhaps in the chains of self-indulgence, echoing the 'me-generation' of society. But the two-edged sword of the gospel cuts through the barriers and divisions and injustices of our world. Unless our communities begin to show this, we have no gospel at all, we have nothing to say; but if we begin to take up the cross of Christ, and to reflect the fullness and hope of the gospel message, then our world will be very interested. It is time either to walk sadly away, or simply to roll up one's sleeves and get started.

APPENDICES

A STUDIES FOR GROUP DISCUSSION OR PERSONAL REFLECTION

The following are three sections of material designed for either group or private use and based on Bible passages, with questions that relate both to the passage and to the material that has been discussed in the book. There is also a biblical meditation for potential peacemakers which, I hope, will motivate and stir those keen to put into practice some of the lessons of this book. The GNB version has been quoted throughout the studies.

STUDY ONE – FOLLOWING THE WAY OF THE CROSS

Read John 13:1–17

1   In John 13:1 we read that Jesus 'knew that the hour had come for him to leave this world' and that he 'had always loved those in the world who were his own, and he loved them to the very end'.

   How does Jesus show his 'love to the end' in this passage?

   What vital lesson is he teaching as his time on earth is drawing to a close?

   Does the timing of the feet-washing incident in relation to the urgency of Jesus' own timetable at this point tell us something about the importance of this incident?

2   The way of the servant is soon to become the way of the cross. Look up Mark 8:34 and discuss what it means to 'take up the cross' and follow Christ.

3   Verse 3 says, 'Jesus knew that the Father had given him complete power . . . So he rose from supper . . .' etc.

How was the feet-washing a sign of his power? What does it teach us about God's way of power?

4 Look at Isaiah 42:1–4 and consider how Jesus saw his role and in what way the body of Christ should be carrying on this ministry.

5 Taking up the cross and denying oneself means a turning upside down of the values of the world – we are freed from those values and that wrong way of thinking. Consider what this means in practice:

a. *In your own church*

    (i) In its treatment of people who come. Does your church value people equally? See James 2:1–5.

    (ii) In the church's (and your own) spiritual aims. What are your spiritual aims? What is more spiritual: is it to be more 'powerful' in terms of abilities and gifts or to be more humble – more of a servant? See Matthew 7:21–23. Discuss true spirituality in relation to obedience, servanthood and the current tendency to hero-worship certain Christian teachers, leaders and evangelists who are spiritually 'powerful'.

    (iii) In worship. In Micah 6:6–8 there is a discussion about worship and v.8 gives the key to a right attitude to worship. A right attitude to worship in church should lead to right actions outside church; as v.8 makes clear, worship is not just what we do in a service, it is something to be lived out.

To consider: Is your church's worship leading to lives of obedience? What has your church done about the rich world/poor world divide, apartheid, unemployment, the nuclear issue, etc?

For personal meditation: What have you personally done about these institutionalised sins?

b. *In society*

    (i) What should be the role of the serving Christian and the servant church in the community? To bear in mind: What are we converted for? Conversion is not the end of a journey! Nor are we converted simply to get others converted. We become Christians in order to live lives honouring to God. This should be reflected in attitudes and actions that assert the dignity of others. We must learn to see people and society through the Father's eyes. This should affect:

○ Our attitude to our career and the way we advance it. Discuss whether you are 'serving' in the job you do. If you do not have a job, consider the role of 'service' within an unemployed context.

For young people not yet embarked on a job or career: Discuss the kind of work that 'serves' society rather than jobs that simply preserve injustice or endorse personal selfishness.

○ Our attitude to money and possessions. Discuss what a Christian attitude to money and possessions should be in the West when two-thirds of the world is in poverty. What is the servant role in this?

STUDY TWO – FREEDOM FROM OPPRESSION

Read Luke 4:16–21
The God of the Bible is the God who constantly reveals himself in action – by setting people free, by bringing salvation. In the Old Testament the great saving event was the Exodus – the freeing of the children of Israel from slavery in Egypt: 'Now I have heard the groaning of the Israelites, whom the Egyptians have enslaved, and I have remembered my covenant. So tell the Israelites that I say to them, "I am the Lord; I will rescue you and set you free from your slavery to the Egyptians . . . I will make you my own people and I will be your God. You will know that I am the Lord your God when I set you free from slavery in Egypt"' (Exodus 6:5–7). So the key factor in the old covenant was freedom from oppression, and by this action the Jews could recognise the character of God who had chosen them.

So it is in the new covenant that Jesus sets us free from the slavery of sin. In Luke 4:18–19 Jesus asserts that he has come to 'proclaim liberty to the captives' and 'to set free the oppressed'. The sin is both our own personal sin that holds us back from being fulfilled and also institutionalised sin – the sin of unjust systems, the sin of the poverty trap. This is the liberating message with which Christians have been entrusted and which reveals the character of the God who has chosen us. 'The God of the Bible is the God of liberation rather than oppression; a God of justice rather than injustice; a God of freedom and humanity rather than enslavement and subservience; a God of love, righteousness and community rather than hatred, self-interest and exploitation' (Allan Boesak).

1 In the light of these comments list some places or situations of oppression and poverty and consider what it means to proclaim the gospel in this context.

2 List the factors which stop people from being free in our own society (i.e. both in terms of personal sin and sinful structure and injustice).

3 In Isaiah 9:6–7 the coming of the Messiah is foretold in familiar words that we hear each Christmas. Jesus is described as the Prince of Peace – the one whose kingdom will 'be at peace'. His rule will be based on 'right and justice'. At his birth the angels proclaim the possibility of 'peace on earth' (Luke 2:14). The word *shalom* or peace is a word that does not simply mean the absence of conflict. It means the establishing of right relationships in the community – the right relationship between God and people and between person and person. Consider how Jesus shows this 'healing' role of the kingdom in practice. List examples of right relationships being restored in Jesus' own ministry and captives being set free (e.g. Luke 4:31–37).

4 The worship we offer in church must lead into action in life. Look at Isaiah 1:15–17; Exodus 22:21–22 and James 1:27. These show us something of the compassionate nature of God. How is your church meeting the specific call to care for widows and orphans?

5 In *Revolution Through Peace*, Dom Helder Camara says, 'I used to think when I was a child that Christ might have been exaggerating when he warned about the dangers of wealth. Today I know better. I know how very hard it is to be rich and still keep the milk of human kindness. Money has a dangerous way of putting scales on one's eyes, a dangerous way of freezing people's hands, eyes, lips and hearts.'
   Discuss the problem of wealth in relation to the above quote and the story of the rich young man in Matthew 19:16–23. What are the implications of Matthew 19:23 on *a*. Our own personal giving and lifestyle? *b*. The way in which church resources are used?

6 How should Christians be bringing pressure to bear on our government when overseas aid is going down in real terms and arms spending is going up? In what practical way can this be done?

7 Consider the style of the birth of Jesus, how it identifies with

the poor and how it sets the scene for Luke 4:18–19. It is the way of the servant, clearly leading to the way of the cross. The message of Christmas and the incarnation is lost most years in a blitz of romance and self-indulgence – how can the local church make the birth of Jesus 'good news to the poor'?

STUDY THREE – THE EFFECT OF THE GOSPEL

Read Luke 19:1–10

This lovely little incident in Luke's Gospel shows the working out of both evangelism and social action in the context of Jesus' own ministry. The very fact that Jesus accepts Zacchaeus so readily transforms him. So it should be with us – as we recognise that God has accepted us we should respond in love to him and to our neighbour. This is exactly how Zacchaeus responds – he gives half of his possessions to the poor and where he has been specifically dishonest he recompenses four times the amount.

1   What does Jesus' own response to this incident (v.9) tell us about the nature and effect of salvation?

2   Jesus met Zacchaeus at his point of need. Zacchaeus longed for acceptance – he was rejected by his own people because his job meant cooperating with the occupying Roman army. Christ's acceptance of him immediately brought a response – he gave to the poor. What implications does this have for our evangelism? Would we have tried to 'preach' Zacchaeus into the kingdom? Are we really living the kingdom as Jesus taught it with all its social implications? (See also 1 John 3:17.)

3   In the light of chapter seven of the book, we in the wealthy West have a need to respond as Zacchaeus did and repent of a lifestyle lived at the expense of two-thirds of the world. How can we show this repentance in practical action?

4   An obedient life has an evangelistic impact. Read Philippians 2:5–8 and discuss the importance of the lifestyle and attitude necessary for the evangelistic impact.

5   John Stott talking about 'the great commission' says, 'I now see more clearly that not only the consequences of the commission but the actual commission itself must be understood to include social as well as evangelistic responsibility, unless we are to be guilty of distorting the words of Jesus.' What implications does this have for your own local church?

6 What is the 'good news for the poor'? In answering this, consider the behaviour of Jesus, e.g. Matthew 11:2–5, and the following quotation:

> The Kingdom stands as a new order of life: the new humanity and the new creation which have become possible through the death and resurrection of Jesus. This new order includes reconciliation with God, neighbour and nature, and therefore, participation in a new world. It involves freedom from the power of sin and death, and consequently, the strength to live for God and humanity. It encompasses the hope of a more just and peaceful moral order, and thus it is a call to vital engagement in the historical struggles for peace and justice. (Orlando Costas, *The Integrity of Mission*)

7 In the light of 1 John 3:17–18, can we claim that the Christian church is showing the love of God in action and bringing good news to the poor when one considers the injustice and poverty in the world? Discuss what you can do about this in your own church and in your own life (both in terms of this country and overseas).

A BIBLE MEDITATION FOR POTENTIAL PEACEMAKERS

1 **Read Isaiah 58:1–10**
The 'religious' are criticised most in the prophets – whether Isaiah, Amos or Micah, for not allowing worship to influence their lives.
How can we live out true fasting in practical ways? Pray to be a reconciler.
Meditate on how to live out a 'just' life.

2 **Read Matthew 5:1–16**
Pray about your own role as a peacemaker (v.9). Then pray about how to let your light shine (v.16).

3 **Read Galatians 3:28**
The gospel breaks the barriers between black and white, powerful and weak, rich and poor, male and female. Ask forgiveness for any barriers you may have endorsed, so denying the work of Christ's gospel, and pray to see your natural prejudices and to reject them. Use the prayer at the end of chapter ten from the Lima Liturgy.

Jot down your personal response to these Bible passages and this time of meditation, e.g. how you will respond in practical ways.

FINAL PRAYER
Father, you sent Jesus into the world to bring a new order – to turn the world upside down. Inspire and motivate me with your Holy Spirit to join him in the task of sharing the gospel of reconciliation in your wounded world. In Jesus' name. Amen.

B TRAVELLING COMPANIONS AND PERSONNEL ON TOURS

HAITI

George Hoffman (Tear Fund)
Tony Neeves (Greenleaf)
   Shown around by Wess Stafford (Compassion) and Lynette Walters (Compassion), among others.

UGANDA

Richard Bewes (now Vicar of All Souls' Church, Langham Place, London, also Chairman of African Enterprise UK)
Lillian Clarke (Road Manager and adviser)
Dave Hofer (sound man)
Enoch Kauma (driver and guide in Uganda)
   Shown round by Bishop Misaeri Kauma, Bishop Festo Kivengere and Kalunji John, Diocesan Youth Officer, among others.

INDIA

Steve Rand (Tear Fund)
Tony Neeves (Greenleaf)
   Shown round by H. P. George (Discipleship Centre), Barry Mackay (World Relief, Canada) and Matthew George (Eficor), Wai and Rose Sin Hu. Vijayan and Premila Pavamani, among others.

SOUTH AFRICA

Tony Neeves (Greenleaf)
  Shown round by Howard Cooper (Tear Fund South Africa), Dr Ivan Toms (Empilisweni Sacla Clinic, Crossroads), Zeph Myathi, Pam McLaren and Bro Walton (all at Ngezandla Zethu – With Our Hands – a handicraft project in Zululand), among others.

KENYA

John Muggleton (Greenleaf – cameraman/producer)
Stephen Lynas (Greenleaf – stills cameraman)
Paul Vigars (sound recordist)
  Shown round by John and Jenny Lawford (Tear Fund East Africa), among others.

SUDAN

John Muggleton (Greenleaf – cameraman/producer)
Stephen Lynas (Greenleaf – stills cameraman)
Peter Novell (sound recordist)
Mark Raffills (Tear Fund, New Zealand)
  Shown round by Magdy Makrum (Fellowship for African Relief) and David Bainbridge (Fellowship for African Relief), among others.

NORTHERN IRELAND

Broken Land Tour personnel:

  Trevor King (promoter)
  Lynas Lacey (sound man)
  Roger Brown ⎫
  Mervyn Jones ⎬ (road crew)
  Andrew Percy ⎭
  Peter McArter (driver)
  Martin Wroe

C DISCOGRAPHY

Most of Garth's songs featured in this book are available on record or cassette. Albums that relate to material in this book and that are currently available are:

PORTFOLIO

Road to Freedom
Oscar Romero
How Hard
On and On
A World of Difference
Namirembe
Record of the Weak
Nero's Watching Video

A Child is the Future
Broken Land
Living Under the Mercy
Litany for Africa (prayer for
    South Africa version)
May you Live to Dance (on
    your own grave)
Light a Candle in the Darkness

ALIEN BRAIN

Alien Brain
My Best Friends Are All Poets
    (& they're living on the
    dole)
Broken Land
Mark of Cain

A Child is the Future
Oscar Romero
Water Off a Duck's Back
Light a Candle in the Darkness
Take Me to your Leader
Robot Clock

ROAD TO FREEDOM

Road to Freedom
Freedom Fighter
Water, Water
Nero's Watching Video
No one is an Island

Namirembe
Rainbow Over Kampala
So Much Better
Zachariah The Zulu
Living Under the Mercy

RECORD OF THE WEAK

A World of Difference
Record of the Weak
Walk in His Shoes
Thunder Like a Lion
The Dust of Death
On and On
A Future and a Hope

Tropical Night
The People of the West
    (Amos Rides Again)
How Hard
Love Song for the Earth
Freedom Tree

THE BEST OF GARTH HEWITT (1973–1978)

Includes 'That's Why We're Here' and 'The Father's Song'.

With the exception of *Record of the Weak*, which is available only through Tear Fund, all are available through Word (UK) Ltd., 9 Holdom Avenue, Saxon Park Industrial Estate, Bletchley, Milton Keynes MK1 1QU.

D VIDEOS

Garth's trips to Kenya and Sudan (chapters five, six and seven) are featured in a Tear Fund video, *A Candle in the Darkness*. The video also includes a sequence of eight songs at the end, some filmed on location in Africa. The songs are:

Broken Land	Litany for Africa (Famine in
The Sky that Wouldn't Weep	Africa version)
A Child is the Future	Nero's Watching Video
Peace at Christmas	Light a Candle in the Darkness
Namirembe	

Garth's trip to India (chapter three) is featured on the Tear Fund video *Cliff in Kenya* in two reports, one called *India (On the Road to Freedom)*, and one for children called *Water, Water*. Both videos are available from Tear Fund (see 'Useful addresses').

E USEFUL ADDRESSES

This is a list of some of the organisations mentioned in the book, plus useful addresses for additional information:

Tear Fund and Tear Craft
100 Church Road
Teddington
Middlesex
TW11 8QE
01 977 9144

Tear Fund supports the work of Christian partners in the developing world with grants and personnel for relief, development and education projects. Through meeting material need within a Christian framework Tear Fund provides a ministry to the whole person.

African Enterprise	African Enterprise has a ministry of evangelism, reconciliation and practical caring for those in need. It works with teams of evangelists throughout Africa supporting the local churches. It is committed to bringing healing among estranged communities and to caring for refugees, drought-affected farmers, victims of injustice, widows and orphans. It is the vision of Bishop Festo Kivengere, who heads the East African side of the work, and Michael Cassidy, who heads the Southern African side.

African Enterprise
5 Crown Close
London
E3 2JQ
01 980 2571

African Enterprise has a ministry of evangelism, reconciliation and practical caring for those in need. It works with teams of evangelists throughout Africa supporting the local churches. It is committed to bringing healing among estranged communities and to caring for refugees, drought-affected farmers, victims of injustice, widows and orphans. It is the vision of Bishop Festo Kivengere, who heads the East African side of the work, and Michael Cassidy, who heads the Southern African side.

Greenleaf Advertising
and Creative
Marketing Limited
D'Arblay House
10a Poland Street
London
W1V 3DE
01 439 6351

Greenleaf works in advertising, design, creative marketing and verbal and visual communications. It has its own film company (Greenleaf Films) for documentaries, videos and a/vs. Greenleaf – born out of a concern for biblical justice – aims to work with any organisations who are working for a better and more just society to help them to do their job more efficiently.

Traidcraft
Kingsway
Gateshead
NE11 0NE
091 487 3191

Traidcraft is a company working with small groups providing fair employment around the world in places where work is short and the poor are often exploited. It is an initiative by Christians working for fairer trading between the poor countries of the 'south' and the rich 'north'.

The Greenbelt Festival
11 Uxbridge Street
London
W8 7TA
01 221 8336

Greenbelt is an arts festival that works from a Christian viewpoint. Held at Castle Ashby over the August Bank Holiday with an attendance of around 25,000. It has a commitment to the creative arts and to the justice and peace issues. Both Garth and Martin Wroe are on the executive committee.

Oxfam
274 Banbury Road
Oxford
OX2 7DZ
0865 56777

Oxfam works in over seventy countries around the world, mainly through small scale self-help projects aiming to improve health, agriculture and community development. It also aims to raise awareness of justice issues.

Evangelical Christians
  For Racial Justice
12 Bell Barn Shopping
  Centre
Cregoe Street
Birmingham
B15 2DZ
021 622 6807

Aims to link Christians together to challenge the ways racism has become embodied in the laws and institutions of Britain, and also to raise awareness of unconscious attitudes of racial and cultural superiority among Christians and to encourage joint action between black and white Christians for justice and peace.

Christian Aid
PO Box 1
240 Ferndale Road
London
SW9 8BH
01 733 5500

Christian Aid is involved in development, relief and education regarding justice and poverty. A wing of British Council of Churches.

The Anti-Apartheid
  Movement
13 Mandela Street
London
NW1 0DW
01 387 7966

Coordinates support against apartheid. Organises boycotts, pressure for sanctions, etc.

Christian CND
22–24 Underwood Street
London
N1 7JG
01 250 4010

Specialist section of Campaign for Nuclear Disarmament working with churches for peace and disarmament.

World Development
  Movement
Bedford Chambers
Covent Garden
London
WC2E 8HA
01 836 3672

Exists solely to campaign for the political changes needed in Britain's policies towards the Third World. Politically has cross-party support and the support of the churches and the major aid agencies.

173

Evangelical Peacemakers 59 Harold Street Hereford HR1 2QU 0432 55724	Links together the growing group of evangelicals opposed to nuclear weapons.
Amnesty International 5 Robert's Place London EC1 0EJ 01 251 8371	Campaigns for the release of prisoners of conscience worldwide.

Catholic Fund for
   Overseas
   Development
   (CAFOD)
2 Garden Close
Stockwell Road
London
SW9 9TY
01 733 7900
	Development, education and relief agency concerned with the causes of poverty and injustice.

Also mentioned in the book:

Compassion	A US Christian childcare and family development agency.
World Relief	A Christian relief and development agency, based both in Canada and in the US.

Eficor – The Evangelical
   Fellowship of India
   Commission on Relief
	An Indian development agency, one of the partners with whom Tear Fund works.

F THE AMOS TRUST

Because of the journeys that Garth has made which are featured in this book, many further invitations have come, largely from countries in the Third World. These are invitations both to sing and share the gospel through concerts, and also to observe and put a spotlight on a particular need or part of the world by songwriting. Garth is being pressed hard to take up some of these invitations and indeed has started doing so.

Naturally these are countries that are in no position to pay even basic expenses, yet from the point of view of ministry they are, without doubt, some of the most worthwhile opportunities. The requests are for concerts that share the gospel in its fullness, taking up the issues of reconciliation, justice and peace, which are at its very heart. These are events to challenge the uncommitted and to encourage and teach those who are already disciples.

Another aspect is that of encouragement of Christian artists in their own countries. Garth has been involved in encouraging artists from a surprising number of Third World countries, and he has a particular concern that artists should be allowed to develop art which works from a Christian viewpoint and which is rooted in their own culture and not 'colonised' or 'imperialised' by western values.

The Amos Trust has been set up specifically to help Garth take up these opportunities. The Trustees are from Garth's home church (St Saviours', Guildford). The Trust welcomes 'investors' to support Garth's ministry financially and in prayer. They receive a regular newsletter with details of Garth's tours, items for prayer and news of how the money is being used. The Amos Trust supports Garth's ministry full-time for up to three months a year. It aims to build support groups who pray and give to this work so that Garth knows that he goes to take up these tremendous opportunities with the backing of a committed group of friends.

The invitations that the Amos Trust would support come into three categories:

1 Visits to the Third World.
2 Visits to other parts of the world where fees and expenses cannot be paid, e.g. Poland.
3 Work in the UK or Europe which may be very worthwhile but cannot pay, e.g. prisons, inner-city venues, etc.

It will also occasionally support Garth in writing or working on certain special projects.

Garth's own commitment in his music and ministry is very much to the biblical themes of justice, peace and reconciliation, and sharing the tremendous healing breadth of the gospel. Ron Sider (author of *Rich Christians in an Age of Hunger*) has commented, 'Garth's music pulsates with a biblical passion for justice and *shalom* rooted in Christ's cross. If a major biblical movement for peace and justice emerges in the late twentieth century, it will be due in significant measure to the consecrated artistic talents of artists like Garth Hewitt.' It is for this reason that the trust has been called 'Amos', after one of Garth's favourite verses, Amos 5:24, 'Let justice roll on like a river, righteousness like a never-failing stream!'

Garth has already completed two tours for the Amos Trust, one to Poland and another to Kenya, and at the moment has outstanding invitations from Uganda, the Sudan, Nigeria, Malaysia and India.

If you would like to know more about the Amos Trust and become part of this ministry, then write to Jane Stevens, The Amos Trust, PO Box 117, Guildford, Surrey GU2 5PY.